CHASING DAYLIGHT
SEIZE THE POWER OF EVERY MOMENT

ERWIN RAPHAEL MCMANUS

THOMAS NELSON
Since 1798

NASHVILLE   DALLAS   MEXICO CITY   RIO DE JANEIRO   BEIJING

Library of Congress Cataloging-in-Publication Data

McManus, Erwin Raphael.
    Chasing Daylight : dare to live a life of adventure / Erwin Raphael McManus.
      p. cm.
    ISBN-10: 0-7852-8113-4
    ISBN-13: 978-0-7852-8113-9
    1. Christian life. I. Title.
BV4501.3 .M375 2002
248.4—dc21   2002010353

Printed in the United States of America
08 09 10 11 12 RRD 16 15 14 13 12

TO KIM

In a moment two become one.
Two lives become one heart.
Two roads become one path.
Two journeys become one adventure.
With you, one moment has become a lifetime.

CONTENTS

ACKNOWLEDGMENTS

SOME MOMENTS ARE SO BIG YOU CANNOT SEIZE THEM by yourself. This book certainly qualifies. So many people stepped through this moment with me and stayed the course until the mission was complete. This project has merged several teams together. I would like to thank Thomas Nelson Publishers for believing in my message and bringing me on board. Thank you, Mike Hyatt, Brian Hampton, Laurie Dashper, and everyone else at Nelson who has served us so graciously. Thank you also to my friend and agent, Sealy Yates. I don't know where you find the energy, but your passion has certainly fueled the success of this project. Every day in Los Angeles I bask in a pool of creativity known as Mosaic. Without this unique community my dreams would remain thoughts and not realities. I am forever indebted to the elders, leadership team, staff, and congregation of this wonderful community of faith and imagination. Especially I would like to thank from Mosaic Dave Auda, who inspired me to write on this topic; Holly Rapp, who moves me from storyteller to author; and Noemi Martinez Bary, who lifted words into images. While I dedicate this book to my life partner, Kim, there is no part of my life that is left untouched by my children, Aaron, Mariah, and our daughter in the Lord, Paty. In many ways they live the book with me.

Finally, words cannot do justice to the level of gratitude I feel toward the God who created us. What a gift He has given us. He created us to live, not simply to believe. To follow Him is to experience, to explore, to discover. Thank You, Lord Jesus, not only for who You are, but for whom You created us to become. So now let us not waste even one moment. Let's face forward and pursue the prize set before us. New eyes will be needed to see this path, but once begun, we will know the exhilaration of seizing our divine moments.

Unleashing the Spirit of Creativity,
Erwin Raphael McManus

"As long as it is day, we must do the work of him who sent me. Night is coming, when no one can work. While I am in the world, I am the light of the world."

— Jesus

John 9:4–5

FORESHOCK

Rumblings are more felt than heard and certainly never seen.
They come to you through the soles of your feet into the depth of
   your soul.
Only then do they open the eyes of your heart.
They speak of a shift that is about to take place.

— Kembr

The Perils of Ayden

Ayden felt still the tyro when Maven gave him his first choice. Shouldn't first he practice on decisions of little weight?

Why would someone as wise as the Maven entrust him with so great a gift?

Was it really true that the riches of all men and kingdoms rested in him? That the good of all stood hanging in the balance?

And how could all of time be bound to one moment?

Even so he could not decline this invitation. This choice was not his to make. His birthright brought both privilege and responsibility.

The journey chose him, but the adventure was his to choose.

To choose is to know the pleasure of freedom, or is it the freedom of pleasure?

— Entry 203
The Perils of Ayden

1

CHOICES

CHOOSE TO LIVE

DEEP INTO THE NIGHT I WAS WALKING DOWN A DARK street in the city of San Salvador under the care of a night watchman who was returning me to my home. No more than six or seven years old, I somehow slipped through the fortress-like security of my grandparents' home and found my way into the dangerous street outside. Later, Papi Hermelindo and Mami Finita even attempted to wait up with a camera to document my escape. Interrogating me was of no value since I had no recollection of the event. I was a sleepwalker going places in my dreams where my body insisted on following. All I would ever remember was dreaming that I could fly, that I was going places that I had never seen but somehow knew awaited my exploration. Waking up always carried with it at least some small disappointment. Such a great divide between dreams and reality—between dreams and life. How in the world is the real thing supposed to compete with what you can conjure in your imagination? Not that life was bad, but it wasn't a dream.

But it didn't stop there. It wasn't just that the dreams made sleeping more attractive than living. The dreams invaded my waking hours as well. It wasn't enough to be a sleepwalker; I was also a daydreamer. I was a citizen, if not a captive, of my imagination. The places I could go, the things I could do, the person I could become were far more compelling than the life I was living. Yet even when I was playing it safe, there was an adventurer scream-ing to be set free.

As I grew, I used books to feed my dreams. I would feed my longing to join a quest through the journeys of endless heroes. Whether it was an ancient odyssey or a futuristic enterprise, I would find adventure through their experiences. But this would only intensify my craving rather than quench it.

There was a voice screaming inside my head, *Don't sleep through your dreams!*

Ever heard that voice? It calls you like a temptress to abandon the monot-ony of life and to begin an adventure. It threatens to leave you in the mundane if you refuse to risk all that you have for

SOMEHOW WE ALL KNOW THAT TO PLAY IT SAFE IS TO LOSE THE GAME.

all that could be. If ignored, the voice dims to silence. Yet every now and again, like a siren, she sings and begins to woo you back. She awakens within you dreams and longings you put to bed long ago. It is rarely a conscious action to choose to exist rather than to live. For most of us we are simply lulled to sleep. But there is no rest in this condition. To sleep through your dreams is to choose a life of restless nights and unfulfilled days. To avoid the pain of fear, doubt, and dis-appointment we have numbed ourselves from the exhilaration of a life fully lived.

We are all haunted with the fear of living lives of insignificance, and we all hear the voice that tells us we can live the dream. Somehow we all know that to play it safe is to lose the game. By def-inition an adventure is "an undertaking or enterprise of a hazardous nature." In other words, it comes at great risk and at significant cost. And life as God intends for you to live it is nothing less than an adventure. You were created for both pleasure and purpose. You might be thinking, *I'm not sure if I really want to undertake an enter-prise of a hazardous nature. Is a life of adventure really worth the risk? Is it really necessary?* Yes, you can choose to play it safe, you can choose to settle for less, but never forget this: You were born to live a great adventure; You were created with a divine destiny; You are called to fulfill a great mission. You were designed for a unique purpose. Now you are called to live it out.

In this I think God has been either terribly misunderstood or tragically misrepresented. All God seems to be known for is legalism, rules, judgments, commands and wrath. In fact, Jesus calls us to live a life of unimaginable adventure. It begins the moment we choose to follow Him. It is no less than to pass from existence to life. Though we are not taken out of time and space, we are translated into an entirely different dimension of living. Jesus tells us that He is the portal into this life and the quest that follows. Jesus describes Himself as a door, a gate, a portal. In other words, an escape hatch. He has come to free us from a meaningless existence and liberate us to a life filled with adventure. He has come to lead us out of the mundane and into the extraordinary. Strangely enough we find it hard to trust Him, while all the time He has been trying to lead us out of the dark dungeons we have created for ourselves and let us run free in the light of day. When we come to Him, he translates us into an entirely new realm of living. His promise is that in Him we will find the life that our hearts have always longed for. Jesus was crucified as a criminal, but what His accusers didn't know was that He was planning and fulfilling history's most extraordinary prison break.

When we open our lives to Him, we can live our lives wide open. We are translated from one reality into another. We are now forever in relationship with the One who is the source of love, life, and freedom.

Everything that we will explore in the pages to come echoes the invitation of Jesus to come and follow Him. He is inviting us on a divine quest. He's calling us to be spiritual pioneers, explorers, and adventurers. To respond to this calling is to accept that you will be a sojourner relinquishing the security of being a settler. To follow Him is to choose to forever be an alien and stranger in this world. You will never be the ideal citizen or even a permanent resident of this planet we know as earth.

TIME TRAVELERS

I have always been fascinated by the concept that H. G. Wells developed in his work *The Time Machine*. At least in my lifetime his imagination has proved to be timeless. *The Time Machine* has gone from literature to small screen and finally to major motion picture. I imagine that H. G. Wells has groomed an entire generation fascinated by time travel. While space travel has become a reality in the past fifty years, time travel seems to be destined to elude us forever, except for one important detail—we are all time travelers. Although we are ill-equipped to survive in space, we were perfectly designed to travel through time. Moving through moments is as natural as breathing. There are, of course, limitations. We cannot travel backward, and we can travel only one moment at a time. Nevertheless, we are all time voyagers leaving history in our wake, pioneering into the future.

In the most recent interpretation of H. G. Wells, one point is made with inescapable emphasis: even with a time machine you cannot change the past, so change the future. Madeleine L'Engle made me hopeful that somehow we would find a wrinkle in time, but so far my experience tells me that time is straightforward, which leads us to the importance of chasing daylight.

Jesus was also fascinated with time. He should be; He came up with the idea. Imagine being the eternal God now walking among your creation within the confines of time and space. Yet while you would think Jesus has all the time in the world, He instead has the greatest sense of urgency. His eternal perspective drives Him to seize the power of every moment. He knows that history has an expiration date. Everything that has a date of birth has a time of death. That doesn't mean that everything ends. You, for instance, are designed for eternal life. While your life on this earth was always meant to be temporary, you were created with the intent to live forever in the kingdom of God's love. Yet as real as eternity is, so is time. We are created in time, and our most important work is time-critical. There are things that must be done today, things that you and you alone were created to accomplish. Some of us are wasting our time burning daylight when what we need to be doing is seizing the power of every moment.

TAKE A MOMENT

If you could capture one moment of your life, which one would it be? Some particular moment in the past? A moment of regret? How many of us haven't spent many moments reflecting on moments lost, all the time unaware that moments lost in regret are exactly that—moments lost? If you could take a moment, seize it, and squeeze out of it all the life available within it, shouldn't that moment be in the future rather than in the past? What if you knew somewhere in front of you was a moment that would change your life forever, a moment rich with potential, a moment filled with endless possibilities? What if you knew that there was a moment coming, a divine moment, one where God would meet you in such a way that nothing would be the same again? What if there was a moment, a defining moment, where the choices you made determined the course and momentum of your future? How would you treat that moment? How would you prepare for it? How would you identify it?

HOWEVER MUNDANE A MOMENT MAY APPEAR, THE MIRACULOUS MAY WAIT TO BE UNWRAPPED WITHIN IT.

Moments are as numerous as the stars in the sky and the sands in the sea, and any of them could prove to be your most significant divine moments. Within those moments, a handful will become the defining moments in your life. However mundane a moment may appear, the miraculous may wait to be unwrapped within it. You rarely know up front the eternal significance of a moment. When a moment is missed, you have a glimpse at an opportunity lost. When you dream, you look to a moment still to come. The moment that you must seize right now is the one in front of you. If you begin to imagine all the moments you are responsible for, it can become overwhelming. Yet moments are not independent, isolated, or disconnected. What you do with this moment affects every moment to come. This is your moment. The biblical imagery for a moment is the wink of an eye. In other words, don't blink or you'll miss it.

I look briefly into the concept of a moment in the chapter "Momentum" in my previous work, *An Unstoppable Force*. I make this observation:

I think we need to spend a day with Monet. He had a clear sense of what was hidden in a moment. Most of us think of a moment as something that's stationary, stagnant, and unchanging. We want to capture the moment and stand in the moment. If there's a moment you want to preserve or remember, you take a snapshot.

The genius of Monet is that he saw the moment for what it really was. It was as if he actually read the dictionary and realized that the essence of the words *moment* and *motion* are the same. Monet was a master of light and movement. His paintings were blurred and obscure and yet beautiful and full of insight. If we could somehow see life through his eyes, we would begin to see life as it really is. Our ability to see the world as it really is has been corrupted by the camera. With a turn of a lens or a push of a button, we are able to take the blur out. We've come to see the world through still frames, when in reality life is in constant motion.

Moments move in a timely manner, and time waits for no one. Though it may seem to be the case, time never stands still. And like petals of a rose, moments fall to the

MOMENTS MOVE IN A TIMELY MANNER, AND TIME WAITS FOR NO ONE.

ground once there is no life in them. Moments are to be treasured—not just the moments that you've already lived, but the moments brimming with life. I can say with confidence this is your moment. There may well be many moments waiting behind this one, and though the most significant moments of your life may still be moments away, the moment you're in right now waits to be seized.

JUST A MOMENT

One of the Greek words from which we get the English word *moment* is *atomos*. You can easily see that the words *atom* and *atomic* come from *atomos*. This is the perfect picture of what is hidden in a moment. The image of an atom reminds us of how easily we could miss a moment or even underestimate it. An atom symbolizes the smallest unit of an element. It was considered the irreducible unit. The idea was that you couldn't get any smaller than this, which is why it is so easy to miss your moment. Like atoms, they come in endless numbers and of insignificant stature. They're just easy to overlook and ignore.

At the same time, we have the image of the atomic hidden in the moment. Within the atomic, there is nuclear capacity derived from the rapid release of energy in the fission of heavily atomic nuclei. There is a disproportionate power in relationship to size. Fission is the act or process of splitting into parts. When you seize divine moments, you instigate an atomic reaction. You become a human catalyst creating a divine impact. The result can even be earthshaking.

This is what we find in the life of a man named Jonathan. A person who, through seizing a divine moment, began a venture he would never forget. Through him we will find ourselves at the edge of uncharted terrain with a challenge to live a life of adventure. Jonathan was the son of Saul, the king of Israel. In the first book of Samuel, chapter 14, the Hebrew text opens for us a defining moment in the life of this young prince. With careful detail Samuel painted for us the textures of how to seize divine moments. The characteristics that Jonathan demonstrated I have seen in men and women who have the uncanny ability to capture the moments of life. They are able to take the atom and make it atomic. What for others would become a moment missed, for them becomes a moment maximized. For them life is full of opportunity and endless possibilities. They share with Jonathan a certain approach toward life. Over time I have come to describe these characteristics as "the Jonathan Factor."

WHEN YOU SEIZE DIVINE MOMENTS, YOU INSTIGATE AN ATOMIC REACTION. YOU BECOME A HUMAN CATALYST CREATING A DIVINE IMPACT.

The Jonathan Factor is the explosive result that occurs when we step into a divine moment and unleash its full potential. How we view God dramatically affects who we become. How we understand God to work directly affects the life we live in God. Even the subtle shift from receiving Jesus to following Jesus is significant. The first allows us to remain stationary as God comes to us; the second demands our moving with God. When Jesus walked this earth, His disciples had to keep up with Him. If they were to stay close, they had to choose to leave the life they lived without Him and go wherever He would go. The life of Jonathan reinforces that God calls us to give our lives for something greater than ourselves. The path is thick with mystery, danger, and the unknown. The quest is to live the life God created you to experience. The journey begins right now—in this moment. And whatever you do, don't underestimate what you may find.

ENJOY THE MOMENT

While I was writing this book, I was rudely interrupted by life. I had an incoming call from the East Coast on my cell phone from a person I had never met. He was a referral from a friend I had helped come to faith several years before. She had met him and found him to be on an intense quest for God. On her suggestion that he call me, we began a long-distance conversation about a spiritual journey. Very quickly into the conversation I expressed how difficult it is to have so important a conversation over the phone. He concurred and immediately suggested that he fly from the East Coast to Los Angeles so that we could talk face-to-face.

Frankly, it was a really busy time in my life. Between leading Mosaic—our community of faith in the heart of Los Angeles—and writing this book, I was squeezing in weekly trips across the country. My family had just requested my increased presence in their lives, so I had cleared my calendar to have extra time with them and, I hoped, finish the manuscript before the deadline. Yet one thing I know about my family is that they can always make time for someone searching for God. So I invited him to stay in our home, and I encouraged him to come as quickly as he could. He seemed a bit surprised that we would invite a stranger into our home, but joyfully accepted our invitation. It was as if he knew there was a window of opportunity and he didn't want to miss it. I later learned that during his flight out he was reading an early manuscript of this book that I had given our mutual friend, and he was clearly determined to seize his divine moment.

One week later, Aaron and I picked up this professor of international policy and brought him into our family. We enjoyed him immensely, and our talks about God convinced me that he had become a genuine follower of Christ. Then he got all weird on me. He asked me if I would baptize him on Sunday. I explained to him that since we rented facilities, we did not have an indoor baptistery, but I would be happy to baptize him either in the ocean or in our pool. I mentioned the ocean only in passing. I never intended to take him to the beach at that time of the year. For LA, fifty degrees is cold, not to mention the water temperature. The Pacific is frigid in the summer and ungodly the rest of the year.

My emphasis was on the pool, but somehow he picked up on this cool nature experience of being baptized in the ocean. He eagerly agreed to be baptized in the Pacific. I referred him to a better way. We have a Jacuzzi. We could warm it up. I could baptize him there. He asked me if being baptized in a Jacuzzi was legitimate. Would it count in the eyes of God? I explained to him that God would accept a Jacuzzi baptism, but it seemed like cheating to him. No, he was clear; it had to be the ocean. I reminded him that it was going to be very cold, that the water would be unbearable, but he was unbending. He would be making a perfect expression of his commitment to Christ. I explained to him that usually I delegated baptism to someone else, but that if he insisted, I would baptize him in the ocean all the same.

So I found myself driving toward Dockweiler Beach on a Sunday afternoon between services. Did I mention it was raining? It was a cold rain, overcast sky, the kind of day Seattle would be proud of. We had no problem finding parking. There was no one manning the ticket booth for the parking area. The beach was empty, as if we had exclusive, private reservations. The locker rooms were locked, and we were forced to change outside in the cold. I had just severely sprained my ankle playing basketball, so I knew I would not even be able to run from the freezing waters to the warmth of my car. The whole experience was destined to be slow and painful.

With just a handful of us there to witness this moment of commitment, my son, Aaron, led us in prayer, and then the two of us made our way into the waters. Man, was it cold! There was only one redeeming feature to the water. It was so cold that it almost instantly froze my legs. I found that quickly there was no pain. After a wave threatened to knock us over and baptize us both, in the calm water to follow, I declared him a disciple of Jesus Christ, baptizing him in the name of the Father and the Son and the Holy Spirit.

When he came out of the water, he looked anything but cold. His eyes were filled with joy and excitement. It was an amazingly warm moment when we embraced in the waters as brothers in Christ. Nothing else seemed to matter then—not the cold, not the pain. All I could do was just enjoy the moment.

The most important moments rarely come at a convenient time. Sometimes you wish that God would check your calendar first. The ironic part is that our schedules get packed with the mundane and ordinary, and we become irritated with God when He interrupts us with the miraculous and extraordinary. The Scriptures are full of stories about people who were rudely interrupted by God. We read them and long to have the kind of adventure experienced by those men and women. Yet when God interrupts us, are we willing to respond on a moment's notice?

STUCK IN A MOMENT

One of the reasons that we are unprepared for the moment before us is that we're stuck in a moment behind us. The 2002 Grammy Award–winning rock album was U2's *All That You Can't Leave Behind*. Positioned right after their hit song "Beautiful Day" is a song titled "Stuck in a Moment You Can't Get Out Of." Side by side they paint a picture of both our opportunity and our dilemma. A beautiful day is out there to be seen and experienced, but you will be tragically unaware of it if you're stuck in a moment you can't get out of. Bono and the Edge write these words:

I never thought you were a fool
But darling, look at you
You gotta stand up straight, carry your own weight
These tears are going nowhere, baby
You've got to get yourself together
You've got stuck in a moment and now you can't get out of it
Don't say that later will be better
Now you're stuck in a moment
And you can't get out of it

The song drives to this conclusion:

And if the night runs over and if the day won't last
And if your way should falter along the stony pass
It's just a moment
This time will pass

Each song is accompanied by a symbol. The symbol for "Stuck in a Moment" is four arrows pointing inward at one small dot. Has this ever symbolized your life? One moment in the past continues to haunt every moment of your life. A moment in your history that steals from you all the moments in the future. Is there a moment you keep reliving again and again? To relive the past is to relinquish the future. If you are willing to let go of the past, then you are ready to step into the future. When you choose to remain stuck in a moment, you become incapable of seizing divine moments.

I know how sticky a moment can become. We're not talking about Post-its, but tar pits. I had stuff that wouldn't let go of me because I wouldn't let go of it. While the world moved on, I kept fighting to live in the past. Remember, though we are time travelers, we were designed to go forward, not backward. When you keep traveling backward, it tears away at your soul. Studying history can be a powerful tool for launching into the future, but living in the past is an enemy of the future.

I was stuck in a moment I couldn't get out of, and it put me in a psychiatric chair by the time I was twelve years old. I carried the baggage that comes with living in the past—depression, despair, isolation. We were not created to walk backward into the future. Just the decision to look forward to the future has a healing power in itself. No wonder God would constantly point Israel to His promise that for them there was always a future and a hope. These two dynamics always come together.

If you're stuck in a moment, turn around, stop looking backward, and dare to look forward. There is a life that awaits you, an opportunity to explore and even create a future. Time was not created with the power to hold you back. And if the future terrifies you, then just take it one moment at a time.

BEYOND A MOMENT

When Halle Berry received her Oscar for Best Actress in a Leading Role for 2002, she was overwhelmed by the moment. Her opening remark, "This moment is so much bigger than me," reminds us that moments are an intersection between the past and the future. For Halle Berry, her moment was a validation of the work and sacrifice of many people who had gone before her. At the same time, it was the door through which she believed future minority actors would be able to pass into new opportunities. Moments are not independent or disconnected realities. Moments carry the momentum of the past and fuel the momentum for the future.

MOMENTS CARRY THE MOMENTUM OF THE PAST AND FUEL THE MOMENTUM FOR THE FUTURE.

Guy Pearce, who played the lead in *The Time Machine*, also starred in another film called *Memento*. In *Memento* he plays a character who has no short-term memory. He is the true existentialist. All he has is the now. He lives essentially without any past and, as a result, without any future. His solution to his dilemma is to tattoo clues on his body so he knows what to do next.

Learning from the past informs and prepares us to seize divine moments. At the same time, looking to the future positions and guides us to move into the moment with confidence. The present moment is where the past and the future collide, and within a moment there is monumental potential. That's the mystery of a moment. It is small enough to ignore and big enough to change your life forever. Life is the sum total of what you do with the moments given you. One definition of a moment is "the period of time during which someone or something exists or an event occurs." Even the description of a moment moves from very small to epic. Listen to some of the words used to describe a moment: instant, flash, blink, twinkling of an eye, split second, minute, hour, day, chapter, phase, season, age, generation, era, epoch. Contained within the concept of a moment is its potential for eternal ramifications.

A CHOICE MOMENT

The divine potential of a moment is unlocked by the choices we make. Each moment's personal, historic, and eternal value is directly related to the choices we must make within it. If a moment is the gate through which your divine journey begins, then choice is the key that unlocks the adventure. Somewhere in the past the power to make choices was moved from the spiritual to the practical. We have created a dichotomy between being spiritual and living everyday life. We have forgotten that God has created us with the power to choose. He has given us the gift of free will. This capacity is perhaps our greatest expression of being created in the image of God.

The most spiritual activity you will engage in today is making choices. All the other activities that we describe as spiritual—worship, prayer, meditation—are there to connect us to God and prepare us to live. While moments are the context within which we live, choices chart the course and determine the destination. We find in Genesis 2–3 that when God created man and woman, He placed them in a garden of choices. Paradise was full of trees and delicious fruit.

WHILE MOMENTS ARE THE CONTEXT WITHIN WHICH WE LIVE, CHOICES CHART THE COURSE AND DETERMINE THE DESTINATION.

We read in Genesis 2:15–17: "The LORD God took the man and put him in the Garden of Eden to work it and take care of it. And the LORD God commanded the man, 'You are free to eat from any tree in the garden; but you must not eat from the tree of the knowledge of good and evil, for when you eat of it you will surely die.'"

In other words, the Garden is full of endless opportunities for pleasure. Adam could choose from the countless number of good trees, and he was free to eat all the fruit he wanted from the endless selection available to him—with one exception. God stacked the deck for Adam. Every choice but one was the right choice. There was only one wrong choice available, and as we all know, he chose it. In that moment, everything changed. His relationship with God was severed. He had chosen another path, one that did not include the presence of God.

Like Adam, we chart our course and navigate our journey with the choices we make. Our choices either move us toward God and all the pleasure that comes in Him or steer us away from Him to a life of shame and fear. The account tells us that while Adam was hiding, God set out in search for him. This is a great point of hope. Even when we get lost in the jungle, God in His great mercy pursues us and invites us once again to join His divine adventure.

MOMENTARY CONFUSION

My frustration with Adam is this: How could he mess it up when he had everything going his way? After all, every potential choice he had was the right choice, except one. That does sound like paradise to me. Now it feels as if we live in a jungle where there are endless wrong choices, and we are to desperately search for the elusive right one. Thankfully, we will find that this is not at all the case. Right when I'm ready to surrender to what seems to be an overwhelming challenge, I'm confronted by God's perspective on my present dilemma.

In Deuteronomy 30 God spoke to His people:

> Now what I am commanding you today is not too difficult for you or beyond your reach. It is not up in heaven, so that you have to ask, "Who will ascend into heaven to get it and proclaim it to us so we may obey it?" Nor is it beyond the sea, so that you have to ask, "Who will cross the sea to get it and proclaim it to us so we may obey it?" No, the word is very near you; it is in your mouth and in your heart so you may obey it. (vv. 11–14)

In what appears to me to be a very sarcastic tone, God said plainly, "Don't use the fact that you don't know what to do as an excuse, and don't even think about telling Me that it's too difficult and beyond your ability. All you need to know to move forward and seize divine moments is right in front of you."

The Lord continued,

See, I set before you today life and prosperity, death and destruction. For I command you today to love the LORD your God, to walk in his ways, and to keep his commands, decrees and laws; then you will live and increase, and the LORD your God will bless you in the land you are entering to possess.

But if your heart turns away and you are not obedient, and if you are drawn away to bow down to other gods and worship them, I declare to you this day that you will certainly be destroyed. You will not live long in the land you are crossing the Jordan to enter and possess.

This day I call heaven and earth as witnesses against you that I have set before you life and death, blessings and curses. Now choose life, so that you and your children may live and that you may love the LORD your God, listen to his voice, and hold fast to him. For the LORD is your life, and he will give you many years in the land he swore to give your fathers, Abraham, Isaac and Jacob. (Deut. 30:15–20)

God pointed the way to two different paths. One is a journey that parts ways from Him; the other is a journey in which He parts the way. Without ambiguity He defined one as the road to death; the other as the path to life. And if we were still confused, He clarified further, "The LORD is your life." No excuses, no ambiguity. The options are clear, and the journey is determined by something as simple as a choice.

Three powerful, life-changing words passed on from God to us: *Now choose life!* Right now, this moment, put away the baggage from the past, shake yourself free from the fear of the future unknown. Right now, choose life—seize divine moments.

A **DEFINING MOMENT**

Choices unlock divine moments. Some moments are filled with far more significant choices. Some choices in a moment change your life forever. You may be able to go back and recognize one decision you made that has sent your life spiraling ever since. You keep waiting and hoping that the consequences of that past decision will soon come to an end. In the same way, you may recognize that in one moment you made a choice from which you have reaped years of benefit.

As I reflect on my life, it seems that a handful of moments shaped the texture of my entire life. I'm convinced that most of us could summarize our lives around five or six defining moments— moments that if we had chosen differently would have radically altered the trajectory of our lives. For me two of those defining moments were choosing to become a follower of Jesus Christ and deciding to ask Kim to marry me.

I spent the summer of 1983 traveling throughout southern California speaking in different churches. On one of my breaks, I headed to Laguna Beach for some much-needed R & R. I worked my way to the top of the cliffs that overlooked both the marine preserve underneath and the beach renowned for its beauty. I stood there soaking in what I concluded was one of the most beautiful sights I had ever seen and felt the soothing power of waves melodically crashing against the surface of the rocks. It was like watching nature dance, and the sound was its applause.

It was in that moment that I decided to make the commitment I just couldn't seem to make before. I had never seen a good marriage. As a child, I knew all too well the tragic pain of divorce. I knew what it was like to have one parent who was a faceless stranger. I also knew how people who were once in love could bring each other great pain. I was filled with uncertainty about my ability to avoid the same outcome. Was I really willing to commit to someone for a lifetime?

But the moment changed me. I remember thinking that life is going to be full of moments like this—spectacular, breathtaking, memorable. What awaited me was an adventure filled with surprise and wonder. I knew in that moment that I did not want to experience the journey alone and that Kim was the partner perfectly suited to travel with me into the future. The choice in that moment changed everything. My life would never be the same again. There are for all of us defining moments that radically alter the course and content of our lives.

GOOD CHOICE

The power of a moment makes it a source of immeasurable opportunity and hope. No matter what kind of life you've lived, no matter how many wrong choices you've made, the next moment is waiting to give birth to new life.

Perhaps no one illustrates this better than a woman named Rahab found in the book of Joshua. She was a resident of Jericho during the time when Joshua was the leader of Israel. Jericho would soon fall into the hands of God's people. To prepare for their conquest, Joshua sent two spies into the city, and they stayed in the house of Rahab. All the Scriptures tell us about Rahab before this point is that she was a prostitute. That was the sum total of her life. If you've ever observed the life of a prostitute, you would know the word *life* is an overstatement. *Existence, torment, punishment, living dead*—all are better descriptions of the waking hours in the life of a prostitute. What nightmares could possibly haunt her dreams that would overshadow the nightmare that comes when she is awake? Yet in one moment Rahab's life changed forever.

She had heard of the God of Israel. In her own words, she was convinced that "the LORD your God is God in heaven above and on the earth below" (Josh. 2:11). Based on that conviction, she offered to help them if they would save her life and the lives of her family members. The spies agreed and instructed her to tie a scarlet cord in her window. If she did that, all of her family who were with her in her house would be saved. The story tells us, "Joshua spared Rahab the prostitute, with her family and all who belonged to her, because she hid the men Joshua had sent as spies to Jericho—and she lives among the Israelites to this day" (Josh. 6:25).

The family that Rahab saved was not her husband or her children. Those are relationships rarely known in the world of a prostitute. She had no husband or children. She saved the lives of her father and mother, her brothers and sisters, and all who belonged to them. In truth, she had no one who belonged to her. The questions that occur to me are: Where was her family while she was living the life of a prostitute? Where were her father and mother when she needed guidance and direction? Why didn't her brothers and sisters rise up to help her and save her from the life of decadence and destruction? And how could the heart of a prostitute that should have long gone cold still be filled with such compassion for the family she left behind? Surely the only future she was saving was theirs. What kind of future did she really have to save anyway?

Yet we find in this moment not a future saved, but a future created. Rahab found more than protection among the people of God. She found a new family. We are informed later that Rahab married an Israelite. Rahab married a man named Salmon, whose son was Boaz, the husband of Ruth, whose son was Obed, whose son was Jesse, whose son was David, king of Israel.

AT OUR WORST, GOOD IS ONLY ONE DECISION AWAY.

And if you follow the lineage far enough, you find that the blood of Rahab flowed in the veins of Joseph, the husband of Mary, the mother of Jesus. The prostitute Rahab, in one defining moment, through one life-altering decision, began a journey that brought her everything she had lost and more than she ever could have imagined. Like Rahab, we are always just one choice from a different life. At our worst, good is only one decision away.

THE **MOMENT** OF **TRUTH**

Moments come and go, and often the opportunities that lie within them leave with them. Time is a tyrant. It consumes choices left unmade. The only choices that live are the ones that are taken, but there can be momentary delays. The good news is that when you choose the good, when you choose to move with God, nothing can stop you from fulfilling God's purpose for your life.

Have you ever felt that you were making the right choices, but everyone around you was holding God up? That could be how Caleb felt when he had to travel in the company of Israel. Moses asked the leaders of each tribe to select one man who would go and spy out the promised land. Among the twelve were Joshua and Caleb. They were to return and give a report to the people of Israel. I gather that Moses' intent was that the twelve would come back with a report so inspiring that God's people would eagerly move forward. Ten of the spies came back acknowledging that the land was amazing, but their report focused on the negative.

In Numbers 13:27–28 those ten in unison reported to Moses: "We went into the land to which you sent us, and it does flow with milk and honey! Here is its fruit. But the people who live there are powerful, and the cities are fortified and very large. We even saw descendants of Anak there" (those were the giants).

In contrast Caleb spoke up as he silenced the people before Moses and said, "Let us go up at once and take possession, for we are well able to overcome it" (Num. 13:30 NKJV).

The other ten rebutted his conclusion: "We can't attack those people; they are stronger than we are" (Num. 13:31).

The passage goes on to tell us that they spread among the Israelites a bad report about the land they had explored. Their conclusion was, "The land we explored devours those living in it. All the people we saw there are of great size. We saw the Nephilim there . . . We seemed like grasshoppers in our own eyes, and we looked the same to them" (Num. 13:32–33).

The people chose to reject Caleb's affirmation of God's command and promise. They even instigated a rebellion against Moses and began to choose another leader who would take them back to Egypt. That choice was about to cost them the next forty-five years of their lives. In fact, the end result was that all who chose not to proceed would be left behind. A generation would pass, and they would be buried in the wilderness they were unwilling to leave.

Only Joshua and Caleb would live to see the promise fulfilled, which leads us to Caleb forty-five years later. He was eighty-five years old. His friend and partner in the journey, Joshua, was dividing the land. In the middle of Joshua's distribution, Caleb spoke up and reminded Joshua of the events leading up to that day. He looked back to Kadesh Barnea, the place where Israel had a choice to make. It was their moment of truth, and they failed. But not Caleb.

He reminded Joshua,

I was forty years old when Moses the servant of the LORD sent me from Kadesh Barnea to explore the land. And I brought him back a report according to my convictions, but my brothers who went up with me made the hearts of the people melt with fear. I, however, followed the LORD my God wholeheartedly. So on that day Moses swore to me, "The land on which your feet have walked will be your inheritance and that of your children forever, because you have followed the LORD my God wholeheartedly."

Caleb went to explain, "Now then, just as the LORD promised, he has kept me alive for forty-five years since the time he said this to Moses, while Israel moved about in the desert. So here I am today, eighty-five years old!" (Josh. 14:7–10).

In other words, Caleb was reminding Joshua, "I was ready forty-five years ago to take the land, but because God's people refused to move forward, it cost me years of my life. I have been wandering in this wilderness because they would not choose to join this great quest. I've been waiting a long time, but my moment has come."

Caleb then declared, "I am still as strong today as the day Moses sent me out; I'm just as vigorous to go out to battle now as I was then. Now give me this hill country that the LORD promised me that day. You yourself heard then that the Anakites were there and their cities were large and fortified, but, the LORD helping me, I will drive them out just as he said" (Josh. 14:11–12).

Do you hear what Caleb was saying? "I've been waiting for forty-five years for this moment, waiting not just to live in the land, but to fight the battle." It's as if Caleb was warning Joshua, "Don't you consider for a moment giving me some tranquil piece of land already settled. I may be eighty-five, but I'm not ready for retirement. I want the land of the giants. I want the biggest challenge. I want to go where the timid would not dare journey. I refuse to surrender the adventure."

So the passage concluded, "Then Joshua blessed Caleb son of Jephunneh and gave him Hebron as his inheritance. So Hebron has belonged to Caleb son of Jephunneh the Kenizzite ever since, because he followed the LORD, the God of Israel, wholeheartedly" (Josh. 14:13–14).

In your moment of truth what will you choose? Will you choose the wilderness or the adventure? Have you confused the blessing of God with wealth, comfort, and security? Have you considered that God's greatest gift to you is that He calls you to be a pioneer, explorer, and even creator? There are things God does for you and things that God waits for you to do. The journey begins when you choose. Stop wasting daylight. Choose a life of meaningful adventure. When you do, you will live in the epicenter of God's activity.

EPICENTER

Do not stand in the center if you do not wish to be shaken.

There is always danger when the movement comes.

Its force is most powerful underneath the surface, then breaks

   through the hardest of ground.

Epic change moves from the inside out.

— Ayden

The Perils of Ayden

One day Jonathan son of Saul said to the young man bearing his armor, "Come, let's go over to the Philistine outpost on the other side." But he did not tell his father.

Saul was staying on the outskirts of Gibeah under a pomegranate tree in Migron. With him were about six hundred men, among whom was Ahijah, who was wearing an ephod. He was a son of Ichabod's brother Ahitub son of Phinehas, the son of Eli, the LORD's priest in Shiloh. No one was aware that Jonathan had left.

On each side of the pass that Jonathan intended to cross to reach the Philistine outpost was a cliff; one was called Bozez, and the other Seneh. One cliff stood to the north toward Micmash, the other to the south toward Geba.

Jonathan said to his young armor-bearer, "Come, let's go over to the outpost of those uncircumcised fellows. Perhaps the LORD will act in our behalf. Nothing can hinder the LORD from saving, whether by many or by few."

"Do all that you have in mind," his armor-bearer said. "Go ahead; I am with you heart and soul."

Jonathan said, "Come, then; we will cross over toward the men and let them see us. If they say to us, 'Wait there until we come to you,' we will stay where we are and not go up to them. But if they say, 'Come up to us,' we will climb up, because that will be our sign that the LORD has given them into our hands."

So both of them showed themselves to the Philistine outpost. "Look!" said the Philistines. "The Hebrews are crawling out of the holes they were hiding in." The men of the outpost shouted to Jonathan and his armor-bearer, "Come up to us and we'll teach you a lesson."

So Jonathan said to his armor-bearer, "Climb up after me; the LORD has given them into the hand of Israel."

— 1 Samuel 14:1–12

Ayden waited as Maven sat patiently by the fire. His silence only made the time pass more slowly.

What was he listening for? Only the wind dared speak. Would his commission come from the mountain's breath? Would the north or the east call his name?

How would he know when to leave and begin his pilgrimage? How would he know which way to go?

When he could bear it no longer, he chanced to interrupt his mentor and blurted, "When will I begin?"

"Now," Maven replied.

"Then which way do I go?" Ayden could not hide his frustration in his asking.

Maven instructed, "Anywhere there's not a path, yet you find footprints."

Suddenly Ayden realized that all through the night it was Maven who waited on him.

— Entry 392
The Perils of Ayden

2

INITIATIVE

JUST DO SOMETHING

IT WAS A COMBINATION FAMILY VACATION AND SPEAKING engagement. The location was the beautiful beaches of Florida's northern peninsula. My wife, Kim, and our kids, Aaron and Mariah, were looking forward to enjoying the warm waters of the Gulf of Mexico. My assignment was to call several thousand singles to a life of sacrifice as we basked in soothing tranquillity. A tropical storm had just hit the area and left the waters basically unswimmable, but my little boy, Aaron, insisted on going down to the beach. So we walked from our beachside hotel down four or five steps right onto the beach. To my right there were perhaps a hundred or so singles enjoying the Florida sun.

And then I saw him. He had somehow managed to find his way to the water, and now he had begun to find his way back. I had not seen him before, and he did not appear to be a part of the retreat. In fact, it seemed as if no one was even aware of him. He appeared alone in the middle of the crowd. He was a double amputee who had worked his way, with the use of specialized crutches, through the sandy beach. Just as I had noticed him, one crutch slipped, and he fell hard to the sand. Undaunted, he pulled himself back up and began again, only to fall a second time. It all happened in what seemed an instant, long enough for me to see him to my right and choose to turn to my left.

I wish I could say I simply wasn't thinking, but the problem was that I was. I knew if I turned to my right, I would have to do something. So I turned to my left. I gently placed my arm on my son's shoulder, turned him away, and began talking to him to distract him from the scene below. We went a few feet, and I felt sure we were free from any responsibility—until my son stopped me. To my surprise, he said, "I have to go help that man."

No explanation was needed. I knew exactly what he meant. His words pierced through me, and I stood there paralyzed in my hypocrisy. I could only look at him and say, "Then go help him." Several thoughts were racing through my mind. *I had been caught* was one of them. Yet at that point, it wasn't that I was unwilling to go; it was just clear that this was Aaron's moment. I had missed mine. His compassion had moved him to heroism. While Aaron seized his divine moment, I was stuck in a moment I couldn't get out of.

I watched my ten-year-old son run across the beach and, without explanation, begin to pick the man up. I had to wonder what the man was thinking when this little boy grabbed him and his crutch and tried to pull him up. I watched as the crowd turned and saw Aaron's futile effort to help the man back to the hotel deck. Almost immediately I watched the crowd move toward Aaron and the man. Someone picked up the crutches, while others reached down and picked up the man. The group moved as if they were one unit, committed to helping the man complete his journey.

After the group helped him return to the hotel deck, Aaron came running back to me, and there were tears in his eyes. He looked at me with his innocent conclusion: "I couldn't help him. I wasn't strong enough." He couldn't see that no one would have helped the man if he had not taken the initiative. My sense of shame was overwhelmed by my deep sense of pride in who my son was becoming. I explained to Aaron that his strength carried the man. It was because of him that the others came to his aid.

IMPROVING ON NOTHING

Have you ever faced this kind of moment—a moment filled with opportunity and yet you let it slip away? Have you ever known you should go to the right, but you went to the left? Has it ever been in your power to do good, but you chose instead to do nothing? You didn't choose to do evil; you just chose not to get involved— you chose to be neutral, to be a nonparticipant, to do nothing. For years the dominant focus of Christianity has been on the elimination of sin from our lives. Yet on the whole, I find the choices between good and evil to be pretty clear in the minds and hearts of those in relationship with Christ. It is not here that we become paralyzed. Once I am willing to turn from my sin and live a life that honors God, what do I do next? How do I distinguish between all the good choices in the world?

You would think that having unlimited options would be the platform for freedom, but that is often not the case. We have put so much emphasis on avoiding evil that we have become virtually blind to the endless opportunities for doing good. We have defined holiness through what we separate ourselves from rather than what we give ourselves to. I am convinced the great tragedy is not the sins that we commit, but the life that we fail to live.

WE HAVE PUT SO MUCH EMPHASIS ON AVOIDING EVIL THAT WE HAVE BECOME VIRTUALLY BLIND TO THE ENDLESS OPPORTUNITIES FOR DOING GOOD.

You cannot follow God in neutral. God has created you to do something. It is not enough to stop the wrong and then be paralyzed when it comes to the right. God created you to do good. And doing this requires initiative. There is a subtle danger of hiding apathy behind piety. Getting rid of the sin in your life? Great. Now it's time to do something.

James, the half brother of Jesus, once concluded that if you know what is right to do and you do not do it, it is sin. He gave us God's perspective on inaction—what we could perhaps call living a passive life. Have you ever stopped to reflect on how your life would be different if you chose to go to the right rather than to the left? If you chose to get involved, to get your hands dirty, to risk failing

GETTING RID OF THE SIN IN YOUR LIFE? GREAT. NOW IT'S TIME TO DO SOMETHING.

in an attempt to do something meaningful? Can you look back on your life and remember moments that would have changed your life forever had you made different choices? Some moments have a lifetime of momentum; other moments appear mundane and later prove to be monumental. Every moment is priceless, unique, and unrepeatable. And within the countless numbers that make up our lives, there are divine opportunities awaiting us.

This may sound too simple, but the abundant life that Jesus promises is ushered in through the choices we make in the ordinary moments of life. Even those who change the world, who make a difference in history, who live life rather than simply watch it, have at least one common characteristic among them: they do something. They don't just watch; they don't just think about it; they act. When we react, life invades our space, intrudes on our comfort, interrupts our apathy, and forces us to respond. But to react is different than to act. We react when we are *forced* out of neutrality. We act when we *refuse* to stay there. If there is one secret to seizing divine moments, it is that you must take initiative.

A MOMENT IN TIME

In 1 Samuel 14, a prophet named Samuel recorded a short period in the history of Israel. He told us about a king's son named Jonathan.

Jonathan is an unusual character in the history of Israel in that his father was the country's first king. And though one would expect that Jonathan would inherit his father's throne, that privilege was essentially taken from him and given to the son of a shepherd named David. It would be easy to assume that was an indictment of Jonathan. His place in history could have been nothing more than the son who could have been king. Instead, we find that Jonathan was the farthest thing from a loser rejected by God. The annals of his life describe a noble with the courage and character that inspire others to greatness. Jonathan never resented God's selection of David as king. He became David's greatest ally, even when his father, King Saul, became David's adversary.

Samuel gave us a glimpse of this unique individual who did not allow his circumstances to limit the impact of his life. The Israelites were at war with the Philistines. You might remember Goliath, the great Philistine warrior. The Philistines were warrior giants who inhabited the land that God had promised Israel. They were also a people described by God as both idolatrous and wicked. It was God's desire to establish Israel as a nation that would reflect His character. Through them He would bring all the nations to Himself. The Philistines were convinced that their gods were more powerful than the God of Israel, and so a war raged between them.

Jonathan's father, as king, was the leader of Israel's army. Due to a variety of circumstances we'll get into later, attacking the Philistines seemed to be imprudent at that time. In the middle of the night, Jonathan awakened his armor-bearer and said to him, "Come, let's go over to the Philistine outpost on the other side." He began to demonstrate what we will describe as the Jonathan Factor.

Samuel detailed how Jonathan did not tell his father, but sneaked out while the six hundred warriors with them were asleep. The circumstances that led Jonathan to make his decision expose a dilemma we all face. As warrior-king, Saul had the responsibility to lead the charge. He had been commanded by the Lord God to engage in battle and was promised a sure victory; yet Saul turned left when he should have turned right. While in the middle of the war, the Philistines, with their ominous weaponry and their massive armies, brought fear into the hearts of the Israelites. Saul was instructed to wait seven days, until Samuel arrived, to bring an offering before the Lord. Instead of doing what he knew was right, Saul acted out of fear and arrogance. Instead of waiting on Samuel to come and fulfill his priestly duties, Saul demeaned the process established by God and took things into his own hands.

This is a stark reminder that while God leaves us with many choices to make, when He has spoken, the one right choice is to obey. Even the most spectacular rivers have banks that direct and guide them. In the same way, where there is freedom, we must initiate, and where there are boundaries, we must honor them. The book

IN THE SAME WAY, WHERE THERE IS FREEDOM, WE MUST INITIATE, AND WHERE THERE ARE BOUNDARIES, WE MUST HONOR THEM.

of Hebrews reminds us that one of the primary evidences of spiritual maturity is the ability to distinguish between good and evil, or to know the difference between right and wrong. I am thankful that God has not made these boundaries mysterious or unknowable. Yet there is a greater challenge beyond this. It is the ability to seize every divine moment. Which leads us to what we might call the pomegranate dilemma.

THE **POMEGRANATE DILEMMA**

Samuel described the dilemma that faced Jonathan. He told us that Saul was staying on the outskirts of Gibeah under a pomegranate tree in Migron, and with him were his six hundred soldiers and also

Ahijah, who was the priest of the Lord. In other words, all of the political, military, and religious authority needed to act was under Saul's direction. Earlier, Saul was too impetuous to wait on Samuel to invoke the blessing of God before they went to battle. Now he was paralyzed and afraid to engage in the very same battle. There is a tragic reality that many times the very things that God blesses us with become the obstacles to seizing divine moments.

Saul had been entrusted with all of the authority and resources of Israel, yet had misused his God-given privilege. So while the Philistines prepared to crush the Israelites and claim the land for themselves, Saul and his armies slept under the pomegranate tree. The urgency that once caused him to act impetuously was gone. But it was more than a lack of urgency that moved him to inaction; he didn't trust God's leadership. His response to having done something wrong was not to do something right, but to do nothing at all.

Having worked more than twenty years with many large and established organizations, I have seen the pomegranate dilemma again and again. Those who hold the authority and resources of the kingdom are all too often more motivated to make sure they do not lose them rather than to make sure they are used properly. It would not be unfair to describe an organization that does this as a spiritual Enron. Any organization that consumes more than it creates will collapse in the end.

I was walking through downtown Atlanta with two of our team members from Mosaic. Most of the city was empty or at least indoors since it was so cold, yet down one of the streets was a long line of hip twenty-year-olds. We were immediately curious to see where they were going. Their line led to an old but uniquely designed building. It was obviously packed and had a large crowd waiting to get in. It was a blues club. Its vibrancy and distinct menu of music seemed to be a magnet for young urban professionals.

And then I saw an old sign that gave a glimpse into its past. It was a former Southern Baptist church. But more than that, it was the former facility of a church that invited me to consider becoming pastor more than ten years ago. When I read through their strategic plan for the future, it was clear that it was an attempt to hold on to the past. Even with a prime location within walking distance of the Omni, they were unable to forge a new future. Without question the congregation had a great and memorable past. There was certainly a day when their attendance was high and their giving was generous and overflowing. It would have never crossed their minds that there would be a day that their community would come to an end. Like thousands of other congregations in the Western world, they held so tightly to what they had that they could not open their hands to receive what was to come.

The greatest danger that success brings, aside from arrogance, is the fear of losing what has been gained. The courage and willingness to risk that breed success are endangered after success is obtained. In the end these very institutions are the ones that have an adversarial relationship with urgency and risk. Urgency is characterized as impetuousness, while risk management is defined not as taking the right risk, but as avoiding risk altogether.

THE GREATEST DANGER THAT SUCCESS BRINGS, ASIDE FROM ARROGANCE, IS THE FEAR OF LOSING WHAT HAS BEEN GAINED.

This can also be true about how we live our lives on a personal basis. The more you move with God-given urgency, the more God seems to bless your life. The more God blesses your life, the more you have to lose. The more you have to lose, the more you have to risk. The more you have to risk, the higher the price of following God. In some twisted way, God's blessings to us can become our greatest hindrances to seizing divine moments.

When Kim and I were in our twenties, had no kids, no house, nothing to tie us down, it was easy to respond to even the slightest prompting of God's Spirit inviting us to a new challenge. After all, we were not much more than educated nomads. Everything we treasured was essentially contained in our relationship. There was really very little else to consider. Then God blessed me with a job that paid more than $10,000 a year, and then He blessed us with a son. Then He blessed us with a brand-new house. Did I mention the new car and all the great furniture? After ten years of sacrificial ministry, it seemed as if the floodgates of heaven had been opened to us in terms of earthly possessions.

Then His voice came again, inviting us to a new journey, calling us to a new adventure. It sounded wonderful, but there were a few minor glitches to the invitation. The job would have to go, the house would have to go, the retirement would have to go, all of our savings would have to go, and most of the really cool stuff would have to go. We were allowed to keep the kids, which was about to include Mariah since Kim was pregnant. It is not an understatement to say that God's blessings were like an anchor around our ankles. We had received them as we walked with God, yet now they had the potential of paralyzing us and robbing from us the divine moments before us.

As it happened for Kim and me, with every benefit, we must embrace both responsibility and risk. One of the wonderful side effects of following Jesus Christ is that you get better at living. The practicality of the life of faith is that you begin to make wiser choices. When a whole group of people start living differently because of their relationship to Jesus Christ, the entire community changes. Sociologists call this redemption and lift. For some this has meant literally a journey from the streets to the suburbs. Who of us would not celebrate the power of the gospel to alleviate poverty and give underprivileged people a fresh beginning?

Many of us, though, face a new poverty. We are not living on the streets, but we are stuck in a rut. We are in danger of gaining the whole world and losing our souls. What we have received from God has taken preeminence over the God who has received us. His gifts are for us to enjoy, but not for us to worship. If what He has given us now stands between us, we must once again lay it at His feet. No matter how rich we become, we must always remain poor. We must ensure that while we celebrate the goodness of God, we do not neglect the purpose of God. When we sit under the pomegranate tree protecting the life we have, we risk relinquishing what God really wants for us—to seize our divine destiny. It may not seem like much, but three words separate Jonathan from Saul—three words separate Jonathan from most of us—"Come, let's go." He simply acted on what he knew needed to be done.

WE MUST ENSURE THAT WHILE WE CELEBRATE THE GOODNESS OF GOD, WE DO NOT NEGLECT THE PURPOSE OF GOD.

KNOWLEDGE ISN'T POWER UNTIL YOU ACT

Years ago I was on a road trip with a friend of mine with whom I share a birthday. He is one of the most gifted people I have ever known. Bright and articulate, he is one of those people who seem to have an unfair share of gifts and talents. Yet he was paralyzed about what to do with his life after seminary. There were so many options and opportunities before him, from senior pastor to various ministry staff positions, not to mention the endless requests for him to speak at events and conferences. He wasn't a believer on the bubble; he was deeply committed to Jesus Christ. In fact, he was a passionate and intense follower of Christ. He wasn't having to choose between good and evil. His dilemma was that there were so many good options that it was hard to know which one to take.

His greatest concern was doing something that would go against God's will for his life. He waited with earnestness for God to speak to him in a clear and undeniable way, but nothing seemed to come. The more there was silence, the more he was filled with uncertainty. For some reason, he did not feel he had permission to choose, so he chose not to choose. And so, by not choosing, he was essentially choosing to do nothing.

I gave him the same advice that I have given many others who seemed destined to pitch a tent at the crossroad. I told him, "Just do something."

He seemed shocked at what seemed a callous disregard for the will of God. He responded that he had too much respect for the sovereignty of God to just do something.

I asked him if he thought that Hitler or Stalin had been capable of thwarting the sovereignty of God.

He said, "Of course not."

I pointed out that if men and women who gave their lives for a purpose counter to the will of God could not stop God's purpose in history, how could someone who longs to do God's will and chooses to do something in line with God's character? I told him I had too much respect for the sovereignty of God to think that he or I could mess it up.

One of my favorite stories in the book of Acts is about the apostle Paul. You would think if anyone knew the will of God, it would be the apostle Paul. After all, he was God's instrument for writing much of the New Testament. Paul's unique place in the Christian faith makes him something like a superhero or at least superhuman. Yet what you find is that Paul was as uncertain about which way to go as many of us are in our life journeys.

In Acts 16:6–10, Luke described his journeys with Paul. He

told us how under Paul's leadership it was necessary for the Holy Spirit to keep them from preaching the Word in the province of Asia and then how the Spirit of Jesus would not allow them to go into Bithynia, though they gave it their best effort. It was only while Paul was asleep and received a vision that he finally discovered that he was supposed to go to Macedonia.

In many ways Luke's travel journal is a divine comedy. It tells us that Paul had no idea where he was supposed to be going. At first he was sure Asia was the right direction, and then he redirected to Bithynia. And only when he was unconscious did he finally understand that he was supposed to go to Macedonia. It took the whole Trinity to keep Paul from going to the wrong place. On top of that, while Paul was conscious, he just couldn't get it.

There is some irony that Paul had to be unconscious for God to speak to him. But the point is this: Paul didn't know *where* he was going, but he did know *why*. His compass was the heart of God. He was fueled and driven by the passion and urgency that God had placed in his heart—to take the life and freedom that comes in Jesus Christ to every person on the face of the earth. What God makes clear is that when we're committed to seizing His divine moments, He'll make sure He gets us to the right place at the right time. What God can do through a person who's willing to act is limitless.

One of the most-asked questions among sincere followers of Jesus Christ is, "What is God's will for my life?" We want a detailed map or plan. We want God to spell it out so we can follow the instructions. Too often we want it clear and uncomplicated, but God simply does not work like that. For a lot of us the most spiritual thing we can do is to do something—to turn right when we want to turn left.

FOR A LOT OF US THE MOST SPIRITUAL THING WE CAN DO IS TO DO SOMETHING— TO TURN RIGHT WHEN WE WANT TO TURN LEFT.

So we must move beyond simply choosing between right and wrong. We must resolve not only to leave the path of doing evil, but also to passionately pursue a life of doing good.

The danger is getting stuck in between the two, living your life in the neutral zone. No real evil to speak about, but no great good to be proud of either. This takes us beyond having nothing to be ashamed of to being ashamed if we do nothing. It is rarely counted as evil when we live in neutral. At worst a passive life is only pitied, yet God counts it as a tragedy when we choose to simply watch life rather than live it. Jesus described as wicked the person who leaves his talent unused. When we fail to choose, we choose to fail. You cannot put your life on hold. It moves forward with or without your approval. Choosing not to choose does not put off the problem; it only exacerbates it.

God designed us to move through time with intentionality. Even waiting on God is a proactive activity. Whether it's reflection or revolution, each moment deserves our creative engagement. The apostle Paul told us that when it is in our power to do good, we should do it. This may be the underlying texture of initiative. Others call it proactivity. Years ago when I went to the leadership institute at the Gallup Organization, they described this characteristic as the "drive to execute." It doesn't matter what you call it; it only matters if you do it.

"Do what?" you ask.

Something.

SIDELINERS

I have a confession to make. Most of my life I was a sideliner. I was an observer of life rather than a liver of life. You know what I mean if you're a sideliner too. For instance, at the high school dance I was a sideliner. I watched people on the dance floor, wishing I was one of them. I rehearsed the invitation again and again, "Would you like to dance?" But I could never muster up the courage to try it on anyone. With each song, I would work up my courage, and I knew I was almost there by the time the song came to an end. If what happened inside your head counted, I would have danced a hundred times with a hundred different girls. But in the end, I was still a sideliner.

The same was true in sports. I had a moment or two here and there, but most of the time I was a sideliner watching others play the game while I sat close enough to feel the impact of shoulder pads hitting, yet remained a safe distance away. No, I wasn't in the stands, just riding the bench. I remember during my senior year in high school, one of the football coaches walked up to me during track practice and said, "Erwin, you have the talent, but you lack the confidence. We kept waiting for you to step up." He was right. I was a sideliner.

Sometimes you can even be on the field, in the game; you look like a player, but you're really just a sideliner. In league basketball I would position myself to make sure I didn't get the critical pass so that the game would not be in my hands. It was easier to let someone else take it. I had a uniform on and I would break a great sweat, but I was still a sideliner.

I have a suspicion that there are far more sideliners than we could ever imagine. People who look as if they're in the game, but are really just watching from up close. This is certainly true in the church. Even our architecture betrays us. The pews are set up for observation. A couple of people do all the work, and everyone else watches. It just occurred to me that the pews look and feel a lot like the benches I used to sit on during football season. I guess that would make the balcony the bleachers. In any case, our churches seem to be designed with the resignation that most of us are sideliners and only a few are the real participants.

Unfortunately this is far more true when we leave the building. How many of us consider the work of Christ our personal responsibility? Isn't the minister the person who's paid to care about others? Isn't that why I tithe? Isn't the missionary someone who leaves our church and goes overseas somewhere? Then where does that leave the rest of us? How would your life be different if you understood that everyone that God calls to Himself He puts in the game?

To follow Jesus is to move with God. When you become a part of God's movement, you are a missionary. Every missionary has a mission. The mission gives him both intentionality and purpose. He has no minutes to waste. He is required to seize every divine moment. Is it possible that God longs for this for all of us?

SEIZING DIVINE MOMENTS IS NOT SIMPLY ABOUT OPPORTUNITY; AT THE CORE IT IS ABOUT ESSENCE.

Maybe you've been afraid to get in the game because you're afraid to lose. In the kingdom of God, victory comes the instant you refuse to simply watch life happen and you get in the game. For too many of us, because we fear failure, we are afraid to try. Sometimes we live vicariously through the lives of others. Instead of being life voyagers, we become life voyeurs. I think it's one of the reasons we entertain ourselves to death. We find our romance in *You've Got Mail*, and we fight our battles through William Wallace and Maximus Aurelius. And there might as well be a glass screen between real life and us because the closest we get to fulfilling our life's dreams is watching them. We've accepted our place, our lot in life, as sideliners.

FROM **PASSIVE** TO **PASSIONATE**

When someone near us seizes a divine moment, it stirs something within us. A lifetime of passivity only makes dormant our longing for adventure. A life where endless moments are left buried in the cemetery of unfulfilled opportunities may grow cold, but not dead. Until our bodies return to dust, there will always be a voice crying out within us to move from existence to life. The possibilities that await us in each moment are fueled by the potential God has placed within us. Seizing divine moments is not simply about opportunity; at the core it is about essence. It's about the kind of life you live as a result of the person you are becoming. The challenges you are willing to face will rise in proportion to the character you are willing to develop. With the depth of godly character comes an intensity of godly passion. It is in this process of transformation that we find the fuel to engage with confidence the opportunities placed before us.

For some strange reason many sincere followers of Christ have come to think that their passions are always in conflict with God's purpose. Yet the psalmist said, "Delight yourself in the LORD and he will give you the desires of your heart" (Ps. 37:4). When you draw near to God, God infuses passion. God works through human desires.

In Buddhism the goal of the spiritual journey is the elimination of desire. In Christianity the goal of the spiritual journey is the transformation of our desires. God's intention in transforming our hearts is not the elimination of desire, but something quite different. To have no desires is to be without passion. A person who lives without passion is someone who is literally apathetic. When we delight in God, we become anything but apathetic. In fact, we become intensely passionate. These desires of our hearts are born out of the heart of God. The more you love God, the more deeply you care about life. The more deeply you

IN CHRISTIANITY THE GOAL OF THE SPIRITUAL JOURNEY IS THE TRANSFORMATION OF OUR DESIRES.

care about people, the more deeply you are committed to making a difference in people's lives.

There is a direct relationship between passion and initiative. The more passionate you are, the more proactive you will tend to be (even if you boldly do the wrong thing). Here's where the dilemma lies: this can actually be paralyzing for a sincere follower of Jesus Christ. You don't want to passionately do the wrong thing. You desperately want to do what's on God's heart, not just on your heart. Here's the liberating reality: when you are passionate about God, you can trust your passions. God uses our passions as a compass to guide us. To put it crassly, when you are madly in love with God, you can do whatever you want. I am convinced this may be the best contemporary translation of Psalm 37:4.

There are few things more inspiring than a life lived with passionate clarity. Yet sometimes observing others live that kind of life can leave a bitter taste in the mouth along with the thirst. One of the ways we cope with watching others live the life we want is by concluding that those on the other side of the screen are more talented, more gifted, more fortunate than we are. They have to be different from us; otherwise, that kind of life would be possible for us too. Yet while the glass screen between us in life may insulate us from the dangers we fear, it cannot insulate us from the desires that rage within us. Even sideliners want to live. There is never a deep satisfaction with simply watching life go by. You cannot live vicariously through someone else's life. We were not created to watch from the sidelines. We were created in the image and likeness of God, to hear His voice and journey with Him.

Those men and women whose lives you admire, who somehow seem to live life to the fullest, would probably be the first to tell you they are no different from you and me. It's not about talent or giftedness or intelligence; it's about moving out of passivity into activity. It is about a refusal to live a life in neutral and to value the irreplaceable nature of every moment. For these individuals, time is a priceless commodity. It is about treating each day as a gift from God and recognizing that every moment lost can never be regained. The Jonathan Factor results in initiative born out of urgency. You see it in the person for whom every moment counts.

ARMCHAIR QUARTERBACK

For nearly ten years the focus of my life was working with urban poor people. In one of those experiences essentially ten of us were in the midst of overwhelming human need. The number of meaningful things that needed to be done was endless. I couldn't begin to count how many times people would come up and say, "Pastor, someone needs to do something about . . ." With every identified problem, there was a recommended program, service, or ministry that needed to be started. It seemed as if the congregation's job was to find the problems and recommend the solutions, and my job was to get all of them done.

Somewhere along the way, out of desperation, I began to ask the same people who identified the need to become a part of the solution. The response was almost always uniform: "Oh, no, not me. I just felt it was important to point out the need." This is where sideliners are particularly lethal. They have so much time to watch life go by that they have a great view of all the problems, which inspires them, especially when they assume their role in life is to point out what's wrong. They conclude that their contribution is at best to suggest solutions and then sit back and evaluate how well we are doing. If you're not careful, sideliners can move you by need, control you with guilt, and leave you dead from exhaustion.

Before I knew it, I felt like the guy who kept spinning the plates, trying desperately to make sure none of them fell and shattered. I had all of these important programs going that would quickly lose momentum as soon as they lacked my attention. Now I have to admit, the church members were wonderful cheerleaders. They would always commend me for implementing all the services that needed to happen. Most of the time when I started a ministry that someone else identified as a need, it would cease to exist the moment I detached from it.

Like an epiphany from heaven came the insight that changed my ministry. One day when someone insisted that a certain service needed to be provided, I simply looked him straight in the eyes and said, "If God has placed this on your heart, He must want you to take responsibility to make sure it happens." I went on to explain that my role would be to help ensure that he was equipped to be able to succeed; God had not called me to do what He had placed on that person's heart; He burdens the heart that He calls.

In other words, God rarely shows you the problem so that you can tell someone else about it. More often than not the very people who insisted that a program needed to be started didn't care enough about it to invest their energy or to give their lives for it. Once they were pressed to take ownership over the importance they attributed to the problem, the problem quickly diminished in importance.

Others responded differently. The realization that the burden placed on their hearts might be God's compass for their future direction was absolutely exhilarating.

FIRST MOVE

God transforms us into spiritual activators. I was once taught that in the way of the samurai, he who makes the first move is the one to die. There may be more truth to this than we would ever imagine. Yet this is the way God's kingdom advances. Someone must make the first move. Someone must be willing to lay his own life on the line. Someone must be willing to do what must be done.

Over the past few years, the teachings of Henry Blackaby have had a tremendously positive impact on a large number of people. His insight that we should look for what God is doing and then get in on it has moved us to greater obedience. Yet I think it's important to add that while God has been working in human history since He breathed life into Adam, there are many things yet to be done, and beyond this, many things yet to be begun. There may be another question that needs to be asked beyond "What is God doing?" and that is this: "What is God dreaming?" Is there something that God wants initiated and He's waiting for someone to volunteer? In Isaiah the Lord said to His people, "Open your eyes! I am doing a new thing. Will you even be aware of it?" (Isa. 43:19).

In every movement, no matter how big or small, someone went first. Isn't the essence of spiritual leadership someone who is willing to follow God first and closest? Sometimes we're like a bunch of children who are afraid to walk through a darkened hallway. The conversation sounds much like our adult dilemma: "You go first. No, you go first." The pioneers, the divine adventurers, always go first.

THERE MAY BE ANOTHER QUESTION THAT NEEDS TO BE ASKED BEYOND "WHAT IS GOD DOING?" AND THAT IS THIS: "WHAT IS GOD DREAMING?"

ISN'T THE ESSENCE OF SPIRITUAL LEADERSHIP SOMEONE WHO IS WILLING TO FOLLOW GOD FIRST AND CLOSEST?

THROUGH THE WINDOW

When we stand on the sideline side of a divine moment, that moment can elude us because of its simplicity. It can seem so average, so mundane. Everything extraordinary about it may be imperceptible from where we stand. And because of that, when we miss those divine moments, we may not think we've missed anything at all. We may just assume that life is nothing more than humdrum, that there wasn't anything there to seize. That is the greatest tragedy of all.

We can even become jealous of those who seem to have many divine opportunities. They seem destined for greatness. Opportunity is always knocking at their door. We just don't get it. While there may be a door, and there was a knock, it wasn't opportunity knocking; it was the person who saw the opportunity. It would be wonderful if somehow we could see through the window, see life from the other side, get a small glimpse of what today could look like by going through the corridor of opportunity. It's almost as if we live in alternate realities, two dimensions of opportunity, and the choices we make determine on which side we live and experience life. And if it were not enough for us to see all that we were missing, or all the possibilities that were ours, perhaps if we could see all the good that we could do, all the lives that we could touch, it would move us to the other side. We cannot see all that awaits us, and we'll never know unless we step into the moment and unleash what God has in store.

There is a reason why the movie *Dead Poets Society* resonated in the hearts of many people. The mantra of carpe diem captures us all. We must seize the day because within each day there are God-given opportunities waiting to unfold, and every twenty-four-hour period is full of divine moments.

I was reminded of this in a conversation with a friend named Joe White. Joe is perhaps best known for his message on the cross where he carries on his back a cross that would typically take six men to move. Joe has been diagnosed with terminal cancer, and in a recent conversation he reminded me that he was more fortunate than I was. He was clear that today might be the last day he had to live. I could live under the delusion that today is just one day of many still to come. The gift of his cancer was the value of today. Perhaps in a way that few of us ever do, he engages each day fully committed to seize divine moments. The mystery of those moments is that they look so ordinary from the sideline and only become extraordinary when we enter them.

Aldo Caruso is a U.S. immigrant from Argentina. He spent most of his adult life teaching in East LA. For years he hoped someone would create positive opportunities for the underprivileged children in the center of Los Angeles. As an Argentinean, he understood how soccer was central to the culture of Latin Americans.

Aldo suggested that someone should do something to help those children. Then one day it became clear to Aldo that he was that someone. I later learned that Aldo's brush with death through cancer raised his level of urgency and gave him the courage to commit. From his beginning a soccer clinic at a nearby elementary school, to starting a soccer team, to forming a soccer league, hundreds of children, if not hundreds of families, became the direct beneficiaries of Aldo's initiative.

Elaine Chang Fuddenna always seemed moved by the condition of poor people. She never let you forget. She was the kind of person you didn't want to be around because you always knew how much you didn't care. The kind of person you always wanted to be around because you became a better person when you were with her.

But being concerned wasn't enough. She had to do something about it. She started a job program called Job Net. The idea was pretty straightforward—build credible relationships with employers through the reputation of the local church and help individuals who were unemployed and high risk get another chance. Through her initiative, more than five hundred men and women found employment, and instead of looking for a handout, they received a hand up.

As far as I was concerned, Susan Yamamoto had a crazy idea. She was a nurse who wanted to start a health care team. Now that may not seem a strange idea to you, but I knew we didn't have any doctors in our church. And two or three nurses are not really the material from which such a comprehensive medical work could be built. But she was determined. Her husband, Rick, one of our elders, has often told me that his wife's passion and determination surprised even him. Susan would have best been described as quiet and reserved, a cooperative person, but certainly not a leader. Two years later, we now send medical teams throughout the year to work in impoverished communities in Mexico. We also have a year-round health care nurse who works as part of our spiritual community who gives her life to serve her city. Susan started a project that required doctors, and through her commitment to serve others, she began drawing doctors into our community of faith.

A wonderful thing happens to people when they become passionate about something: they become proactive; they take initiative. And the reverse seems to work too. When you begin to take initiative, when you begin to do the good that you see needs to be done, you find yourself growing in passion. When you commit to "just do something," you move in the right direction. Once you're moving in a direction that is aligned with the character and heart of God, you find God's personal mission for your life begins to come into focus.

Not every divine opportunity will create a new ministry or organization, but that really isn't the point. Every divine opportunity is born out of the power to do good. The fuel of doing good can range from passion to compassion to a commitment to serve others. The Scriptures provoke us to do good toward others when it is in our power to do so. And sometimes a simple act of grace toward another human being becomes the window through which God pulls us into His future for us. While God never promises that we'll know everything about the future, or even that we'll live without mystery in the present, He does promise that we can live life to the fullest.

Is it possible that Jesus' promise in John 10:10, that He has come to bring us life and life more abundant, was always intended to be experienced through this adventure? It begins by realizing that God has already told us so much about His will for us that we could spend the rest of our lives simply fulfilling what is already revealed. Do what you know you should do, and you will know what to do. God clarifies in the midst of obedience, not beforehand. It is fair to say that God informs us on a need-to-know basis. The Scriptures give us what we all need to know, and Jesus promises us that His Spirit will lead us if we will follow Him. But as was the case for Nehemiah, whom God commanded to rebuild the walls of Jerusalem, the details didn't come until after he went.

DO WHAT YOU KNOW YOU SHOULD DO, AND YOU WILL KNOW WHAT TO DO. GOD CLARIFIES IN THE MIDST OF OBEDIENCE, NOT BEFOREHAND.

There's an old saying that it's better to try to tame a wild stallion than it is to ride a dead horse. Which one are you more like? The dead horse that needs to be brought back to life, or the wild stallion, filled with passion and desire for life? If you're more like a dead horse, take hope in the One who raises the dead. If you are a wild stallion, run to the One who will not tame you, but will transform you. God's desire is not to corral you, but to set you free. God's compass for life is not information, but truth. The key is not the ability to read God's mind, but to know His heart. It is critical to grow in the wisdom of God, and this journey must be fueled with the passion of God. All the blessings of God without urgency to live for His purpose become a terrible waste.

I love to play chess. When I haven't played for a while, I always choose black. When I lack confidence, I prefer to begin on defense. Let the opponent make the first move. I'll react. But when I get in the flow, when I'm really in the game, I love being white. I choose the offense. I understand the advantage of taking the first move. The individuals who seize divine moments may lack other qualities, but one thing is certain—they take initiative.

TOUCHED BY INSANITY

Several years ago I found myself frustrated when one of the members of our pastoral staff lacked initiative, to say the least. I tried everything I could think of, from trying to encourage and inspire him to creating tighter accountability with intensified consequences, but nothing seemed to work. I called my brother, Alex, who always has great insight and an unusual perspective on everything, and asked him for some advice. He said the problem was obvious. He said, "The guy is normal. That's really the problem. You think everyone wakes up every morning thinking about how to change the world. That's just not where most people are at."

Then I remembered. I remembered watching life from the outside. I remembered wanting to live, but being afraid. It was as if there was a person inside me waiting to be born. He looked like me, but I knew he was very different. He would not be invisible. He would be more than just a watcher. His life would really matter. My soul was experiencing the pain of labor, but I wondered if this person would ever come to life. It was as if I was going crazy. The normal person I had worked so hard to be was being threatened by the person I so desperately longed to be.

I have thought about Alex's insight many times. I must confess I am no longer a sideliner. I do wake up pretty much every morning asking the question, "How can I change the world?" For me it began with a simple change of perspective. I want my life to be defined by what I give. So many moments are lost when we're looking only for what we can get. You can enter into divine moments only when you are willing to serve. There is a mystery in all of this. I suppose no one put it better than Jesus: when you try to keep your life, you lose it. But when you lose your life for His sake, you actually find it.

This change of focus somehow helped me overcome my fears, my doubts, and my insecurities. Life wasn't about me anymore, so all of that became irrelevant. There is no small life when it is given away, no meaningless moments. Even if everyone around you chooses to sleep, you must resist

WAKE UP! GET OUT OF BED. GOD WANTS TO CHANGE THE WORLD THROUGH YOUR LIFE IF YOU'LL JUST DO SOMETHING.

the temptation to join their slumber. Wake up! Get out of bed. God wants to change the world through your life if you'll just do something.

While everyone else slept, Jonathan woke up. He decided he needed to make a difference in his world. Maybe there is a touch of insanity to think that you or I could really make a difference, knowing who we are, that we could somehow change the course of human history. If it's normal to wake up in the morning and just try to make it through the day, then I vote for abnormality. I choose insanity.

Perhaps the goal of this particular chapter is to drive you out of your mind; to make your heart pound against your chest; to cause you to break a sweat, even though your body is not in motion; to have wild and insane thoughts about what a life with God could be like; to throw caution to the wind and follow God wherever He leads you. Wake up tomorrow morning asking the dangerous question, "What can I do today to make a difference in the world?"

Something, or maybe someone, woke Jonathan out of his slumber. When everyone else around him slept, he got up and went. Maybe he echoed to his friend the very words he heard from God, "Come, let's go."

"I'm afraid," he confessed as Maven stood with him in the place where his quest would begin.

"Of what?" Maven asked in his calming voice.

"For this journey. Have I learned all I need to know?" Ayden queried.

"Ayden," he replied, "you know all you need to learn."

"What should I take with me?" Ayden continued.

"Leave all you have and take all you are."

Ayden persisted, "And the path, is it safe to travel?"

Maven looked at him sternly for the first time he could remember and scolded him, "It is not safe to remain! It is not the place but the presence that upholds you! This is your only certainty. Go! Walk where no man has walked, yet you find footprints."

— Entry 709
The Perils of Ayden

3

UNCERTAINTY

KNOW YOU DON'T KNOW

OUR DAYS ARE NUMBERED

Few numbers have as much significance to our present generation as these: 8:46 on 9/11. I was in my car heading toward the Los Angeles International Airport. I was on my way to Denver for a one-day meeting. Driving down the 105 freeway, I chose not to turn on the radio and to instead enjoy the silence of the morning. As I approached the airport exit, I decided to turn my cell phone on and call my wife to say good-bye before I left. The tone of her voice sticks with me more than the words she said. It was as if someone she loved had just died a tragic death. There was a desperation in her words that seemed out of context to me. She began pleading with me not to get on the plane. She said something terrible had happened in New York.

I really couldn't understand what she was saying, something about a plane crashing into the World Trade Center. I couldn't make the connection. No matter how tragic the accident was, what would that have to do with my flight from Los Angeles? But Kim and I have a rule: if she asks me not to go, I don't go. I pulled off the exit and turned my car around to go home. My son, somehow unconvinced that I had changed my course, called me and said, "Please don't go,

Dad. Just don't go." Then Kim said, "Turn on the radio." I learned what we have all learned—that at 8:46 on 9/11 the world changed.

Those of us who have the privilege of living as a resident in this nation have, in many ways, lived in an unreal world. The level of freedom, prosperity, and safety that we enjoy is unknown to most of the world. Our ordinary experience could appropriately be described as surreal to most of this planet. Most of us here really have lived out the American Dream, but along with the dream there has been a delusion. We began to feel as if life had given us certain guarantees. We even built a theology that validated our false sense of security. Peace and prosperity became expectations. Concepts such as sacrifice and suffering were left to describe only those who were living outside the blessing of God.

And then it happened. Two planes crashing into the World Trade Center became our rude wake-up call out of our sweet slumber. A third plane crashed into the Pentagon. By that time, we had the horrifying realization that the commercial airlines had been turned into terrorist missiles. A fourth plane soon crashed near Pittsburgh. That day moved at a frenzied pace. As the pastor of a church, I had much more to do than secure my own family. Added to that complexity was the fact that we are a community in Los Angeles, and two of the four planes that were used in the terrorist attacks were coming to Los Angeles. If LA and New York had, in the past, a unique relationship, it was intensified on this day. We had disorganized prayer meetings in our home and in other homes throughout the city. It was obvious that people felt the intense pain of loss and were struggling with shock and personal fear.

It was not until the next morning that my wife, Kim, reminded me I needed to walk the children through this. I didn't know what to say to my thirteen-year-old son and my nine-year-old daughter. As parents, we always dread having that first talk about sex with our children. But you never even contemplate having to process your children through something like this. Like children all over this country, my kids watched the images of the planes crash into the World Trade Center again and again and again. I could tell at first there was a disconnection from reality. There was a quality about it that seemed not too distant from the unbelievable special effects in movies. But it quickly enough began to seep in, and they understood all too well what was going on.

What would I tell them? How would I reassure them? I knew what I wanted to say. I wanted to tell them that everything would be all right, that they were safe, that this wouldn't happen to them, and perhaps even their most pressing fear, that it wouldn't happen to me in all the flying that I do. Sometimes it seems the key to parenting is lying to your kids. After all, does a nine-year-old girl really need to understand how close death is to all of us? Isn't the truth too hard a reality? Frankly, what I wanted to tell them just wasn't true. I wanted to tell them that everything would be okay. This would never happen to us. God would not allow something like that to happen to our family. I couldn't promise any of those things, and the comfort I wanted to give them wasn't within my power to guarantee.

So I sat down with my family, and we talked about what September 11 had taught us. This is the summary: you have no control over when you die or (most often) how you die, but you do have control over how you live.

That may seem a little too heavy for a nine-year-old, but I was relieved to learn that it made perfect sense to Mariah. It had a ring of truth, and it gave her something to do. She needed to choose how she would live this day.

ON A **NEED**-TO-**KNOW** BASIS

An era of peace and stability has caused us to make wrong conclusions about what the human spirit needs. You would think that what we need is certainty, the promise that everything is going to be all right, the guarantee that we'll be safe. While I, like anyone else, would love to know that this is the life that God would choose to give to my family and me, the security that we often seek is not necessary to living life to the fullest. Sometimes it can actually become the greatest deterrent to seizing divine moments.

Jonathan was certain about some things, and at the same time he was able and willing to operate in the realm of uncertainty. He called out to his armor-bearer and said, "Come, let's go over to the outpost of those uncircumcised fellows. Perhaps the LORD will act in our behalf." You've gotta love that. This is what he was saying in plain English, "Let's go and pick a fight. Maybe God will help."

Jonathan understood that not everything was guaranteed, that you don't wait until all the money is in the bank. There are some things that you can know and some things that you will not know. He went on to say, "Nothing can hinder the LORD from saving, whether by many or by few."

He had such a clear perspective on reality. What he knew for certain was that God was powerful enough to get the job done, that it didn't matter if it was two of them against a thousand Philistines. His father's apprehension to go to war with six hundred soldiers and only two weapons—that's right, two swords—was reasonable, but not enough to excuse neglecting the purpose of God. And so if it was only Jonathan and his armor-bearer and only Jonathan with a sword, he would still move in line with God's mission for them.

Long before, God had spoken through Samuel to the whole house of Israel, "If you are returning to the LORD with all your hearts, then rid yourselves of the foreign gods and the Ashtoreths and commit yourselves to the LORD and serve him only, and he will deliver you out of the hand of the Philistines" (1 Sam. 7:3).

God had promised Israel deliverance from the oppressive hand of the Philistines, and the way He would do it was by raising up an army of men who would trust in God and go to war against the Philistines. Jonathan was clear about one thing: he knew for certain that nothing could stop the Lord from saving, and God could use a lot of people or only a few people. The odds are irrelevant to God.

Jonathan had an unwavering confidence in God's capacity. He had absolute trust in God's character. He seemed resolute about whether God could be trusted. That was settled for him. Jonathan's focus was not, *What is God's will for my life?* but *How can I give my life to fulfill God's will?* He had no certainty concerning his personal well-being. That he was moving in line with God's purpose was the only certainty he needed. He didn't presume upon the fact that God can be trusted by trusting Him for things He never promised. He understood that to move with God is to accept a life full of uncertainties. The Jonathan Factor is expressed when we have absolute confidence in God in the midst of uncertainty and are willing to move with God even without a guarantee of personal success.

Imagine that you are Jonathan's armor-bearer. He wakes you up from a deep sleep, and he tells you to follow him through a series of cliffs for the purpose of engaging the Philistines in battle. And in his invitation he explains that his best hope is that God *might* help you out. If I were the armor-bearer, I'd say, "Wake me when you know." And I think that is what most of us have done. We've gone back to sleep in the shade of a pomegranate tree, willing to set out once everything is certain.

HOW **CERTAIN** ARE **YOU?**

Several years ago I was lecturing at a seminary, and when I was finished, a young student shared with me that she had planned to go to the Northwest to help start a new church. She continued to explain that in the process she had discovered it was not the will of God. I asked her how she determined that, and she said, "The money never came through." I asked her who told her that lack of finances was proof that God was not in it. She said her pastor and her parents. They said that if God wanted her to go, everything would be provided before she left.

Our wealth and abundance of human resources have positioned us to accept a paradigm that provision precedes vision. This has been the foundation of building no-risk faith. This is a tragedy when a part of the adventure is the discovery that vision always precedes provision. I know this may be a

OUR WEALTH AND ABUNDANCE OF HUMAN RESOURCES HAVE POSITIONED US TO ACCEPT A PARADIGM THAT PROVISION PRECEDES VISION.

real stretch, but it is always right to do what's right, even if it turns out wrong. There are times God calls us to do the right thing, knowing that others will respond in the wrong way. Jesus did the right thing when He left Gethsemane where He struggled to embrace the Father's will and began a journey that would lead to the Cross. The consequence to Him was severe. Our response toward His coming was to crucify Him. We should not be surprised that a lifelong journey with God might bring us suffering and hardship. If the Cross teaches us anything, it teaches us that sometimes God comes through after we've been killed!

Though Jonathan did not die when he engaged the Philistines, there is no principle that says everyone who does God's will lives—at least not on this earth. And if you're like me, when I imagine Jonathan at war with the Philistines, he barely broke a sweat. How many of us imagine his battle and find him wounded and perhaps even near death? Yet this is not unlikely. What would be surprising is to engage in this kind of primal warfare and leave unscarred. All this is to say, even when we live, it doesn't mean the victory comes without suffering.

If we are going to seize divine moments, we must accept the reality that we have no control over many things. We have no control over when we die or how we die. We must instead take responsibility for what we do have control over—how we choose to live.

Jonathan wasn't choosing to die, but he was choosing how he would live. He left the consequence of his actions in the hands of God. He chose to do what he knew was right. Again, God was doing something in history, and Jonathan gave his life to it. This realm of uncertainty is the place of miracles. Sometimes the miracle is wrapped around the person we become, the courage and nobility expressed through a life well lived.

Funerals may be the context where the most is said about us that we never hear. Over time you come to realize that it's not so much what is said about you, but who shows up. I have stood in the midst of funerals where no more than a handful of people came to pay respects, and even those seemed to be there mostly out of obligation or duty. Every now and again you step into a funeral that is really more of a celebration. I've had the privilege to step into moments like that. When I attended the service of Maxine Marie Papazian, out of respect for her brother, Dave Mushegan, I was struck by the scene. Although the auditorium was quite large, there was standing room only. I stood in the back and watched as the memorial progressed, and I was caught by surprise at what I saw: both genuine celebration and heartfelt loss. But what really struck me was the response of the people sitting in the back. You expect the people in the front to be intimately engaged in the experience. Those who are family and close friends usually fill the seats and rows closest to the ceremony. Often the back is filled with the polite, but distant, acquaintances. Yet that wasn't the case. Several of us who were standing against the back wall later expressed how deeply we were moved to see virtually the entire chapel equally grieved at the loss of a dear friend. I left wondering who would be at my funeral: Would people care even all the way to the back?

A person's life does not require some extraordinary event to distinguish it. A life well lived can be equally inspiring and its contribution also great. Sometimes that transformation is best seen through failure, defeat, or even death. Other times the miracle is wrapped around how God comes through in the midst of all that uncertainty.

When you move with God, He always shows up. It's just difficult to predict what He will do or how He will do it. If you wait for guarantees, the only thing that will be guaranteed is that you will miss endless divine opportunities—that you can know for certain.

THE **MIRACLE** OF **UNCERTAINTY**

It must have been four years ago when Greg SooHoo, one of our elders, called me to meet him at a nightclub downtown. It was for sale, and he was proposing that Mosaic consider the location for our future worship center. The property was perfect for us in many ways. We could see endless possibilities. We all felt it was the ideal location, especially for a church like Mosaic. I was more than five years into my work in Los Angeles when we were desperately searching for a more strategic location to meet. Mosaic was a community defined in many ways by its creativity, artistry, and love for beauty. Any facility would need to express a commitment to reach the cultural edge through innovation and uniqueness. The nightclub sitting in the heart of Los Angeles would also communicate our love for the city and our commitment to touch the world by reaching its people.

There was just one problem: the property was a few million dollars out of our range. Now I wish I could tell you that we found those millions of dollars or that miraculously the owner gave it to us, but that didn't happen. Sometimes a divine opportunity appears to be missed, but really it's just waiting for its divine moment.

Maybe a year later a Chinese couple, George and Susan Luk, got the property and reopened a nightclub there. They renamed the nightclub the Downtown Soho. The Soho had as a part of its artistic heritage that it was once known as the Glam-Slam owned by Prince. When the Luks purchased the property, Greg SooHoo called me again and suggested we meet them. On my way to meet George Luk, I kept rehearsing in my mind how I would negotiate the use of the nightclub for our worship service. I had no idea whether he would be open to a church in a nightclub or whether we could afford to rent the place. I knew the approach was critical.

When Greg and I sat down with George, it just sort of came out: "We'd like to invoke the presence of the living God to meet people here in this nightclub and become a voice of hope to the city." I have to admit, he looked pretty shocked. There wasn't a lot of subtlety to my approach. He was gracious and asked if he could talk to his wife before giving us an answer. It wasn't even a week before he responded with a yes. Our cost would be around one thousand dollars a month. That amount would cover the janitorial costs, and he added that if we couldn't afford that, just to let him know.

One of the wonderful things about living in the realm of uncertainty is that you find the journey with God is full of surprises. It was at least a year later, sitting at dinner with George and Susan, his wife, that I discovered why they said yes so readily.

ONE OF THE WONDERFUL THINGS ABOUT LIVING IN THE REALM OF UNCERTAINTY IS THAT YOU FIND THE JOURNEY WITH GOD IS FULL OF SURPRISES.

About fifteen years earlier, her mother was gravely ill. They were certain she was going to die. Years before, a missionary in China had given her mother a Bible that she still kept with her. To find some solace in her condition, she opened the Bible and began to read. She stumbled upon Isaiah 38, where Hezekiah, one of Israel's kings during the time of Isaiah, was facing death. God told him to put his house in order because he was going to die and he would not recover. Hezekiah turned his face to the wall, prayed to the Lord, and asked God to spare his life. And God replied that He heard the prayers and He would add fifteen years to Hezekiah's life.

Susan's mother asked her, "What do you think this means?" Susan's hopeful reply was that God was promising that she would live another fifteen years. Then her mother asked her, "What about the next verse? What does that part mean?" Susan said she really didn't know.

Nearly fifteen years later, George and Susan purchased the nightclub. Her mother, having recovered from her illness, was asked to come and see the facility and bless their endeavor. This is a common practice among many Asian families. When her mother walked in, she said that it would be a great place for church. George and Susan explained that it was going to be a nightclub, and she simply repeated her observation that it would be a wonderful place for church.

Which brings us back to the passage regarding Hezekiah. The part they could not explain said this: "I will add fifteen years to your life. And I will deliver you and this city from the hand of the king of Assyria. I will defend this city" (Isa. 38:5–6). So when we walked in and told them that the nightclub would bring hope to the city and set the city free through the presence of God, it fulfilled the other half of the passage.

How could we have ever known the strange work of God in the lives of George and Susan Luk? If we had waited for everything to fall into place before we initiated, we would have never gone. We all want miracles and then spend our lives avoiding the context in which miracles happen. When we seize those divine moments, even though we recognize that we are inadequate for the challenge before us, we experience the power and wonder of God. Certainly not every divine moment is filled with a spine-tingling miracle within it, but every moment is filled with divine purpose. I once wrote to my family these words: "It is the journey together we share and cherish. It is the adventure we have found in His calling. Sojourners each of us upon this divine landscape. Explorers of dangerous mysteries."

Even without the miracles, the adventure would be enough.

BEGINNING THE JOURNEY OF FAITH

For years I have teased my friend Larry. He is an engineer who had a very systematic view of how God works. I was a new pastor and was calling the church to a very dangerous future. I was asking them to leave traditions that comforted them and to move from a location that had given them identity and security. What he wanted from me was a prophetic "Thus says the Lord." He wanted the assurance that that was exactly what God wanted us to do. If I could give him that, he would follow me anywhere. I took him to this experience in the life of Jonathan, and I told him, "Larry, the best I can do is tell you that maybe God will give us success. I just know what we're doing is right." This concept absolutely short-circuited his engineering mind. It's ironic that Larry and his wife, Rhonda, gave up their lucrative careers as engineers and now live in Asia serving the people of China.

The book of Hebrews tells us that faith is being sure of what we hope for and certain of what we do not see, and that this is what the ancients were commended for. It doesn't mean they were presumptuous about God. It means they believed God for everything He promised. So it's important to note what God does promise and what He doesn't. He promises we can be certain about who He is and we can be certain about our relationship in Him, but how the journey plays out is full of uncertainties—the end of the story is not, though. The last chapter of human history has already been written. Jesus wins! And all who follow Him find that all along they have been more than conquerors in Christ Jesus, their Lord. He defeats death, evil, suffering, sorrow, loneliness, and despair, not to mention the prince of darkness and all his demonic cohorts.

SO IT'S IMPORTANT TO NOTE WHAT GOD DOES PROMISE AND WHAT HE DOESN'T. HE PROMISES WE CAN BE CERTAIN ABOUT WHO HE IS AND WE CAN BE CERTAIN ABOUT OUR RELATIONSHIP IN HIM, BUT HOW THE JOURNEY PLAYS OUT IS FULL OF UNCERTAINTIES.

As I have lived this journey of faith and served within the community of faith, I have noticed that faith has two practical dimensions. I describe them as first-dimension faith and second-dimension faith. First-dimension faith is involved when we step out into any area of trust in God outside our experience, but the challenge set before us is clearly in the realm of possibilities. God is asking us to do something that He has done in the lives of others; we just haven't experienced it. Sometimes it's as practical as God calling us outside our personal experience and comfort zone. In church life this dimension of faith evokes a response: "We've never done it that way before." It's not that it hasn't been done; it's just that *we* haven't done it.

Most of life's challenges are a test of first-dimension faith—trusting God with your relationships; trusting God with your finances; trusting God with your career; and making decisions based on His character in the midst of those arenas. The texture of this dimension of faith has everything to do with character. It is about trusting in God's character and God's testing your character. That's why you cannot speak about faith without talking about obedience.

Many times faith is confused with emotion or desire. Faith is then measured by how strongly we feel or believe something will happen. The assumption is that if our faith is great enough, we will get whatever we ask for. In fact, often we're told that if our prayers do not result in an affirmative answer, it is because we don't have enough faith. We simply didn't believe strongly enough. The more consistent characteristic of those who follow God is that their faith is an expression of trust in God. The need is not to work up our faith in God, but to deepen our confidence in God. The promise of Jesus that if we ask anything in His name, He will do it, is fueled not by how strongly we believe in something, but by how well we represent God's purpose and intention. If a prayer's ultimate intent is to fulfill God's will, we can move with confidence, even if God doesn't answer that prayer the way we expect. The more closely we reflect God's heart in our prayers, the more often our requests will match His response.

Jesus said, "If you have the faith of a mustard seed, you can move mountains." He was not saying that you need more faith. He was saying that it takes very little faith to accomplish great things. The critical issue here is that when we become paralyzed in this first dimension of faith, we are often told we just didn't believe hard enough. Yet Jesus was saying the opposite. In most cases, first-dimension faith is about obeying what God has already spoken. It is about building our lives and moving forward with confidence fueled by commitment to God's truth. At the same time, the focus of our prayers must shift away from trying to get God to do what we ask or even

THE CRITICAL ISSUE HERE IS THAT WHEN WE BECOME PARALYZED IN THIS FIRST DIMENSION OF FAITH, WE ARE OFTEN TOLD WE JUST DIDN'T BELIEVE HARD ENOUGH. YET JESUS WAS SAYING THE OPPOSITE.

asking God what He wants us to do; like the early disciples in the book of Acts, we are to ask God to give us courage to do what we already know.

In Hebrews 11, a chapter full of men and women described as people who lived by faith, we find the common characteristic is that God spoke to them, called them on a journey, told them what they must do, and then they did it. The description of Abraham is a good summary: "By faith Abraham, when called [by God] to go to a place he would later receive as his inheritance, obeyed and went, even though he did not know where he was going" (v. 8).

Notice that the dynamic is exactly the same as it was with Jonathan. There were both certainty and uncertainty. What Abraham knew was that God called him to go to a place, and so he obeyed and went. Jonathan was called to be a warrior of God against Philistine oppression. The nuances of how it would work out remained undisclosed. But what he didn't know was everything else! He didn't even know where he was going, and yet he went. Seems ridiculous, doesn't it, to begin a journey when you don't even know the destination? You would think you could at least expect God to tell you that much. But for Abraham, He didn't. He called him on a journey that took him to the realm of uncertainty. He called Israel to a battle they didn't know how they could win. God has done this again and again through human history. He calls us out of comfort into uncertainty. Faith is all about character, trusting in the character of God, being certain in who God is and following Him into the unknown.

FAITH IS ALL ABOUT CHARACTER, TRUSTING IN THE CHARACTER OF GOD, BEING CERTAIN IN WHO GOD IS AND FOLLOWING HIM INTO THE UNKNOWN.

This relationship between clarity and uncertainty is accentuated in the life of Gideon. God called him to deliver Israel from the hands of the Midianites. In God's greeting to Gideon, He described him as a mighty warrior. He called him to go in his own strength and save Israel out of Midian's hands with only the promise that God would be with him. As you might remember, Gideon was not convinced. Twice Gideon placed his infamous fleece before God, asking God for a sign that He would be with him. Each time God graciously responded to him.

When Gideon was finally committed to going, he gathered thirty-two thousand men to go to war. At that point, God remained intimately involved in the process, but it was a kind of involvement we rarely want from God. He told Gideon the victory would be too easy for him, so Gideon was to instruct every man who was afraid to return home. His purpose was to ensure that no one could take credit for the victory at hand except to give glory to God, so twenty-two thousand men left and only ten thousand remained. Talk about moving from confidence to uncertainty! But that wasn't enough for God. He told Gideon there were still too many men. He instructed Gideon to take the men to the water and to sift them according to how they chose to drink: "The ones who lap the water with their tongues like a dog, they get to go home. Keep the ones who bring the water to their mouths with their hands." Gideon was left with three hundred men. Just a bit more uncertainty created by God.

God called Gideon to engage the Midianites with those three hundred men. The book of Judges describes these enemies of Israel by telling us that the power of the Midianites was so oppressive, the Israelites prepared shelters for themselves in mountain clefts and strongholds. Whenever the Israelites planted their crops, the Midianites, along with other enemies, invaded the country. They would camp on the land and ruin all the crops. They would not spare a living thing for Israel. They would destroy all the sheep, all the cattle, even the donkeys that belonged to the people of God. One description tells us, "They came up with their livestock and their tents like swarms of locusts. It was impossible to count the men and their camels; they invaded the land to ravage it." It goes on, "Midian so impoverished the Israelites that they cried out to the LORD for help" (Judg. 6:5–6).

Facing such an enemy, Gideon had been stripped down to three hundred men. Gideon must have had the look of a desperate man sentenced to death when he measured the odds against him. Yet in this case, God guaranteed victory. He even invited Gideon to eavesdrop on the Midianites if he was too afraid to proceed. And he did just that. Once again, God confirmed the direction that He wanted Gideon to move in. Gideon was at last convinced that he was the warrior of God called to deliver the people.

And then God was silent. He didn't tell Gideon what to do next or, more specifically, how to do it. With three hundred men against a multitude you would think God would need to give him step-by-step instructions on how to secure the victory, but He didn't. What we find is that Gideon, certain that was what God wanted done, moved forward in the strength he had, just as God had commanded him. So Gideon took his three hundred warriors and turned them into musicians. They surrounded the Midianites and held torches in their left hands and blew trumpets, which they held in their right hands. And for special effects, they smashed jars at the same time. The Midianites were terrified and turned on each other, which allowed Gideon to seize an easy victory.

YET ONE OF THE WONDERS OF UNCERTAINTY IS THAT IT IS THE ENVIRONMENT IN WHICH GOD INVITES US TO BE CREATIVE.

If this isn't the context for uncertainty, I don't know what would qualify. Yet one of the wonders of uncertainty is that it is the environment in which God invites us to be creative. The journey, which can be described as one from comfort to uncertainty, is intended to be an adventure from calling to creativity. If the only calling you are ever certain of is the one where Jesus calls us all to follow Him, and He would make us to become fishers of men, it is more than enough. He commissions all of us to go and make disciples of all nations. He came to seek and save that which is lost. All of us have a calling to give our lives away for His sake. You can move forward with this mandate on your life.

In John 13, we learn that when Jesus knew that all power had been placed under His authority, He tied a towel around His waist and washed His disciples' feet. Afterward, He instructed His disciples to do the same. His instructions were clear: God Himself has come to serve us. We are now to go and serve the world. If everything else remains uncertain, be clear on this point: there is a calling on your life. There is a level of clarity you can have about what to do next. Serving others functions like a compass in the midst of a fog. The unique way God has designed you—with talent, intellect, gifts, personality, and passions—informs you about how that service will be expressed. But don't look for God to fill in all the blanks. Don't wait for Him to remove all the uncertainty. Realize He may actually increase the uncertainty and leverage all the odds against you, just so that you will know in the end that it wasn't your gifts but His power through your gifts that fulfilled His purpose in your life.

IF EVERYTHING ELSE REMAINS UNCERTAIN, BE CLEAR ON THIS POINT: THERE IS A CALLING ON YOUR LIFE.

First-dimension faith is not only about trusting the character of God, but also about transforming your character. Much of first-dimension faith is about doing the right thing regardless of the circumstance or consequence. It is about having the faith that God will be with you when you do what's right. All too often we compromise character to avoid unwanted consequences. We all have to start here, and so much about seizing divine moments is worked out in this realm.

WHEN **FAITH LOOKS** LIKE **FAITHFULNESS**

I have a dear friend named Shelly Collins who had to make some first-dimension faith decisions. She was in her midthirties and single and, like many of us, looking forward to the joy of marriage. In her many years in Los Angeles, the person that she kept hoping God would bring into her life never seemed to show up. Common sense says you need to stay where there are a lot of compatible men if you want to increase your opportunities to marry one. That was no small factor when she began to consider moving overseas to serve in the Muslim world. Even some of the counsel that she was given reinforced that it was perfectly legitimate to wait to go overseas until God brought her a partner for life. Yet what God was calling Shelly to do was clear to her. He was inviting her on a journey that had some real, practical uncertainties. And so, like Abraham, she obeyed and went, in many ways not knowing where she was going.

During her missionary training in Richmond, a former missionary to Korea had relocated to the U.S. after the death of his wife. His partner in ministry and in life had died of cancer. He was now the supervisor for the training of new missionary personnel. In those few days of training, it became clear to him that God had brought Shelly into his life. When I talked to Steve, he described his magnetic pull to Shelly around two concepts—mission and passion. He met a woman who had a complementary focus of life, and equally important, he was very attracted to her. Shelly could have never foreseen that she would not go overseas without her husband, and she would have never met him if she had not accepted God's invitation to seize her divine moment and live in the realm of uncertainty. Today, Shelly and Steve live in the Mediterranean serving Muslims together.

If you want to seize divine moments, you must accept that you are on a divine mission. Speaking to Timothy, the apostle Paul reminded him of the invitation that Christ has given to us all. He implored him: "Join with me in suffering for the gospel, by the power

IF YOU WANT TO SEIZE DIVINE MOMENTS, YOU MUST ACCEPT THAT YOU ARE ON A DIVINE MISSION.

of God, who has saved us and called us to a holy life—not because of anything we have done but because of his own purpose and grace" (2 Tim. 1:8–9). He also told us in Ephesians 2:10 that all of us are "God's workmanship, created in Christ Jesus to do good works, which God prepared in advance for us to do." In Galatians 5:13, Paul declared, "You, my brothers, were called to be free. But do not use your freedom to indulge the sinful nature; rather, serve one another in love." James said it like this: "Anyone, then, who knows the good he ought to do and doesn't do it, sins" (4:17).

If you're going to embark on a journey with God, you must choose to live a life of godliness. Never forget that we killed the Son of God. Living a godly life can be a very dangerous undertaking. Yes, there is a mystery to faith, but there is also a practicality. First-dimension faith calls us to live in the concrete realities of life. And while God may challenge us to engage in a journey outside our experience, faith in this realm is really dealing only in possibilities.

But these are the critical elements to capture in this realm of faith: there are endless possibilities waiting for us, much of the life that God longs for us to live is just one choice away, and so much of the fullness that Jesus promises us is lost at the character level. When we sacrifice our character, when we choose a path that lacks integrity, we are trying to take life into our own hands. It is a declaration that we do not trust the way of God. We are trying to control what we were never intended to control, and at the same time, we are relinquishing control over that for which we are responsible.

The adventure of faith begins with faithfulness. Being faithful is taking responsibility for the good we know to do. It's about treating even the small tasks before us as important and worth our best effort. Faithfulness is God's kingdom pathway to greater opportunity, responsibility, and adventure. Jesus tells us that whoever is faithful in the small things will be entrusted with more, which leads us to a significant truth—faithfulness is a response to calling. And all of us have been called by God to be faithful. Everyone who has chosen to follow Christ has also been called by God. All citizens of God's kingdom have a calling. You may be waiting for a call from God, and you missed the fact that He has already called you. You were created to reflect His image and to fulfill His purpose. You are the living product of divine intentionality. You are not an accident. You were made on purpose, and because of that, you can know that you have a purpose.

YOU WERE CREATED TO REFLECT HIS IMAGE AND TO FULFILL HIS PURPOSE.

Are you willing to live a life that honors God and reflects His character and leaves the outcome to Him? Are you willing to live by faith and trust Him to be faithful? There will be days on this journey of faith when the outcome will be clear, and you will not like the implications. On those days you must, like Jesus, declare, "Father, if you are willing, take this cup from me; yet not my will, but yours be done" (Luke 22:42).

A **NEW DIMENSION** OF **LIVING**

When we make the choices necessary to live a life that maximizes first-dimension faith, then the fun really starts. If first-dimension faith takes us outside our experience, second-dimension faith takes us outside the explainable. While first-dimension faith sees realities in the realm of possibilities, second-dimension faith sees realities in the realm of impossibilities. In first-dimension faith, the context for miracles is internal. God is working in us and through us. In second-dimension faith, the context is often external. God's hand is clearly all around us.

The victory that Jonathan experienced on that day began with God working through Jonathan and his sword. It is no small thing that one man with a sword can slay multitudes with endless weapons. Then God sent an earthquake, and things got really interesting. I am convinced that God longs to put His fingerprint in our lives, to act on our behalf and surprise us with His magnificence. I am equally convinced that most of the time we do not give God a context in which to do this.

The mundane is not really the best context for a miracle. When we play it safe, we squeeze God out of the formula. If we go only where we know and do what we're certain will succeed, we remove our need for God.

WHENEVER WE TAKE ON A GOD-SIZED CHALLENGE, SELF-SUFFICIENCY IS NO LONGER AN OPTION.

Whenever we respond to God's invitation, our need for God becomes heightened. Whenever we take on a God-sized challenge, self-sufficiency is no longer an option.

While the Scripture is full of first-dimension faith, it's the second-dimension faith that stands out. Daniel lived in the days when Babylon ruled over Israel. Darius was king, and with his rule he brought his gods. Daniel was one of the young Hebrew advisors selected to serve in the king's court. Daniel had achieved a place of great influence and respect until Darius was convinced to make it a violation to pray to the God of Israel. Commanded to pray only to Darius, the king, Daniel refused to comply. Instead he returned to his home, went upstairs to where the window was open, and three times a day got down on his knees and prayed, giving thanks to the living God, just as he had always done before.

Daniel's first-dimension faith was that he prayed every day by the window, even when it was against the law. He did what was right, regardless of the consequence. His second-dimension faith was evident when the king threw him into the lions' den and God intervened and he survived the night. There would have been no need for second-dimension faith in Daniel's life if he had not been faithful in the first dimension.

Many times first-dimension faith creates the context for second-dimension. We must remember that if we're thrown into the lions' den and we get eaten, God is still faithful. This is what makes second-dimension faith so exciting. You know that God will be honored because you have done what is right. We find a list of such men and women in Hebrews 11, beginning in verse 35. After describing many whose faith journeys brought victory in this life, the writer described others whose lives were the victory.

Among those living by faith were those who "were tortured and refused to be released, so that they might gain a better resurrection. Some faced jeers and flogging, while still others were chained and put in prison. They were stoned; they were sawed in two; they were put to death by the sword. They went about in sheepskins and goatskins, destitute, persecuted and mistreated—the world was not worthy of them. They wandered in deserts and mountains, and in caves and holes in the ground." The author of Hebrews concluded, "These were all commended for their faith, yet none of them received what had been promised" (vv. 35–39).

If you're thrown to the lions, of course you hope you'll be there in the morning to celebrate. But if not, you will be in the presence of God, and you will have provided a small kindness to a few hungry lions.

PREGNANT WITH FAITH

If we describe a life of faith through the metaphor of having a baby, then Sarah and Mary become our best analogies for first-dimension and second-dimension faith. Both women had babies. Both became pregnant through the miraculous intervention of God, but of course, how they became pregnant was dramatically different.

Sarah was about ninety years old, and Abraham had reached triple digits. When God told them they were going to have a baby, Sarah laughed. I think she was laughing at Abraham. She knew it was more than unlikely that she would ever get pregnant. She had been barren all of her life and was now well past childbearing years. All they had was the promise of God. Their challenge was first-dimension faith—trust God and do what He said. They, in fact, did not trust God, and Sarah gave Abraham Hagar, his concubine, so that she would bear him a son. Doing that was a common practice in their time, but not how God intended to fulfill His promise to them. They did not trust in the character of God, and they acted outside the character that God desired of them.

Eventually Sarah got pregnant and had a son named Isaac. Abraham and Sarah struggled through first-dimension faith. It was difficult to believe, but it could happen through the natural process and it certainly was in the realm of possibilities. To put it delicately, although they didn't fully believe God, they did not stop trying to have a child. God promised them that they would have a son, but it did require their involvement. Sarah got pregnant the good old-fashioned way.

Mary, on the other hand, is a different story. She was living a life that was pleasing to God, and God chose her in her faithfulness. She became pregnant through the miraculous intervention of the Holy Spirit. It wasn't just outside the realm of experience; it certainly was not in the realm of possibilities. Mary's journey took her outside the realm of the explainable to the world of impossibilities. While everything is possible with God, there are a whole lot of things that are certainly impossible without Him. This is the next dimension of faith. When God intervenes and there is really no human explanation, your life points to God, and His hand is undeniable.

WHEN GOD INTERVENES AND THERE IS REALLY NO HUMAN EXPLANATION, YOUR LIFE POINTS TO GOD, AND HIS HAND IS UNDENIABLE.

It is usually this kind of faith that catches our attention. Men and women with this faith are the ones we typically count as the heroes of faith. In some ways this makes perfect sense. Everyone who's a follower of God is a part of a community of faith. Faith is a requirement for citizenship in God's kingdom. So in one sense, every person who follows Jesus Christ is a person of faith. Yet we all know that there are those who distinguish themselves in this arena of faith. They seem to move naturally in this second realm of experience. They seem conduits for the miraculous. Not all the time, but certainly more than most. Most of us long to have and experience this kind of faith.

The first dimension is, again, the hard task of faithfulness. The second dimension seems to be where all the action is. It shouldn't surprise us that we continuously search for ways to access the second dimension of faith without having to embrace this first dimension of faith, yet they are most often inseparable.

WALKING BLIND

An unusual story in John 9 deals with the healing of a man who was born blind. The disciples were walking with Jesus and pointed out the man to Jesus, not to ask Jesus to heal him, but to engage in a theological discussion. They asked Jesus, "Teacher, was this man born blind because of his sin or his parents' sins?"

A part of Jewish tradition and theology was that human suffering was a result of God's judgment on our sinfulness. Then Jesus explained that neither was the right conclusion: "This happened so that the work of God might be displayed in his life" (v. 3). Then Jesus moved to heal him. And I want us to look at how He healed the man. The account tells us that Jesus spit on the ground and mixed the spit with the dirt and made mud. Then He took the mud and placed it on the man's eyes.

Now it would be bad enough to be a blind man who is the object of ridicule. It would add insult to injury that the disciples of Jesus saw him only as an object for discussion rather than as a human being, needing compassion and grace. But then to have spit and dirt caked onto your face—that would be an act beyond insult as far as I'm concerned. Remember he was blind, not deaf. The man knew exactly what was going on. Any interested observer would have to conclude that Jesus was making a mockery of the man. Even those who held out hope that somehow Jesus' strange methodology would lead to an act of mercy would have quickly abandoned that hope when Jesus dismissed him to go wash himself in the pool of Siloam.

Sometimes we read this passage with too much sanctity. When we interpret the texture of this event to make it feel appropriate, we subconsciously think, *Well, it was God's spit, holy saliva, some kind of sacred mud, a miraculous concoction that only God could understand or create.* But I think this idea does a disservice to the whole experience. The spit wasn't from the "fully God" part of Jesus; it was from the "fully man" side. It was just plain, old spit. And by the way, it had to be a lot of spit. It was mixed in with nasty dirt, formed into mud, and then rudely placed on the face of a blind man who could not defend himself.

Perhaps he thought, *If I go through this humiliation, then Jesus will heal me.*

I can't begin to imagine what was going through his mind when he heard Jesus say, "Go to the pool of Siloam and wash." What would you have done? You are blind. How are you supposed to get to the pool of Siloam? Was He offering His help? Was He providing a disciple to guide you there? I wouldn't have gone anywhere if I had been in his sandals. I would have stayed right there. I would have insisted that He heal me before I left His presence. I might have taken offense, allowed bitterness to grow in my heart, and accused Jesus of insensitivity and callous disregard for my pain.

But the man went. The account doesn't provide the details of how he got there; he just found a way. He washed his face as Jesus instructed, and he went home seeing. His neighbors quickly realized what had happened. The man born blind whose life occupation was to sit and beg could now see. When he was asked who opened his eyes, he explained, "The man they call Jesus made some mud and put it on my eyes. He told me to go to Siloam and wash. So I went and washed, and then I could see" (v. 11).

There is one important note that John made that we should not miss. He highlighted a parenthetical thought that ties this experience together. He explained that Siloam means Sent. It was both by name and by metaphor the place of obedience. When Jesus commanded the man to go to the place called Sent, to leave with his prayers unfulfilled, with his needs unmet, with his questions unanswered, in many ways he left in a worse condition than before. He was a blind man with mud caked on his face moving farther away from the only One who could help him. He could have never fully grasped that his healing would come only in the place called Sent. That if he had refused the journey, he would have lost the miracle.

He is a dramatic example of the interconnectedness of first-dimension and second-dimension faith. First-dimension faith is responding in obedience to what God has already spoken. Then you enter the context for the miraculous—welcome to the second dimension.

How many of us are sitting in front of God with mud on our faces waiting for God to heal us? How many of us have said to God, "Heal me and I'll go"? Is it possible that there is a place you must go to experience the fullness of God in your life? There is for all of us a pool of Siloam, a place called Sent, a journey we are called to where things become more uncertain before they become clear, where our need for faith in God increases with every step rather than diminishes. This journey requires absolute certainty in the goodness of God while at the same time we relinquish our demand to know the details.

STEPPING IT UP

This relationship between faith and uncertainty is inescapable. What required faith for you yesterday may become commonplace for you tomorrow. Although they are still expressions of your faith, they are no longer the challenges that launch you to a new-faith experience. While at first simply trusting God to take you outside your experience is a huge leap of faith, eventually God will expect more of you. Remember, faith is being sure of what we hope for and certain of what we do not see. Once something is a certainty, it no longer requires faith. Do not be surprised that what God asked of you yesterday is insufficient for your journey of faith today.

DO NOT BE SURPRISED THAT WHAT GOD ASKED OF YOU YESTERDAY IS INSUFFICIENT FOR YOUR JOURNEY OF FAITH TODAY.

Moses had just led Israel out of Egyptian captivity. Ten plagues had finally convinced Pharaoh to let God's people go. Now Moses stood facing the Red Sea, with Pharaoh relenting of his decision to free them as he came in hot pursuit of his former slaves. When Moses waited at the banks of the waters, God instructed him to "raise your staff and stretch out your hand over the sea to divide the water so that the Israelites can go through the sea on dry ground" (Ex. 14:16). God allowed Moses to stand on the shore and create the path for His people.

His apprentice, Joshua, was not afforded that luxury. Moses was dead and gone. Joshua, who was once Moses' aide, had become the leader of Israel. He stood at the Jordan River between God's people and the promised land. While Moses was allowed to stand on the shore and watch the waters open, Joshua was given a different set of instructions. This time God commanded them, "Now then, choose twelve men from the tribes of Israel, one from each tribe. And as soon as the priests who carry the ark of the LORD—the Lord of all the earth—set foot in the Jordan, its waters flowing downstream will be cut off and stand up in a heap" (Josh. 3:12–13).

With Moses, God parted the waters, and then the people crossed over. With Joshua, the leaders were required to begin crossing first, and then the waters parted. In my life journey, I have found time and time again that God changes the parameters of my faith. He increases His expectation of me. What it means to live on the edge as your faith begins to develop is not the measure of faith when you walk in maturity. You should expect and desire that God would move from parting the waters while you stand on the shore to calling you to step out into the waters and experience the miracle happening around you. In the first, you watch the miracle. But in the second, you become a part of it. Both experiences were expressions of a journey of faith. Both had amazing similarities, but what God required in the second exceeded what He required in the first. My experience is that as we walk with God, He expands our faith capacity. Is it possible that we could walk with God in such a way that all of life is a second-dimension faith experience? I'm not completely sure, but I know I want to find out.

Even the imagery that God uses incites my hunger to live in a different dimension. There is something profound about the relationship between the waters dividing only when the soles of their feet touch the surface. I see the same relationship in Romans 16:20 where Paul told us that "the God of peace will soon crush Satan under your feet." I have no problem believing that God will crush Satan. What blows my mind is that it's not under God's feet that Satan will be crushed; it's under my feet—our feet. I can understand Satan being crushed under the feet of God. We are told that heaven is God's throne and the earth is His footstool. Those are big feet! Yet the question comes to mind: If the soles of our feet have this kind of cosmic power, what untapped potential has God placed in the rest of us?

A power that comes from God is known only when we walk. Jesus began His public ministry by inviting us to follow Him. There is great comfort in such an intimate invitation, yet we must not forget that God is on a journey that none of us can take without Him. King David expressed it like this: "Even though I walk through the valley of the shadow of death, I will fear no evil, for you are with me" (Ps. 23:4).

The God of light insists on traveling into dark places; the God of peace continuously involves Himself in the wars of men; the God who is good engages the depth of human evil. The only God who can deliver and save at the cost of His own life journeys into the dungeon of human lostness to set free those who would relinquish their chains for life in Him. To follow Jesus is to enter the unknown, to relinquish security, and to exchange certainty for confidence in Him.

MOMENTARY SUFFERING

More than twenty years ago, when I was just beginning my walk with Christ, I came across the writings of the prophet Jeremiah. He was easy to relate to, especially in times of crisis and frustration. Jeremiah gave us a window into his own soul when he yelled at God with unfiltered frustration. He cried out,

> O LORD, you deceived me, and I was deceived;
> you overpowered me and prevailed.
> I am ridiculed all day long;
> everyone mocks me.
> Whenever I speak, I cry out proclaiming violence and destruction.
> So the word of the LORD has brought me
> insult and reproach all day long. (Jer. 20:7–8)

You have to be at the end of yourself to believe in God and talk to Him in this way. Can you imagine shaking your fist at God and saying, "You have deceived me"? He had done everything that God had asked of him. He had been true to the journey to which God had called him. And what was his reward? A life of misery and anguish. A life of pain and disappointment. It should not have come as a surprise to him since from the day God called him, he was warned that the nation would turn against him. He described his reward for faithfulness to God as being ridiculed, mocked, insulted, and reproached all day long. He was mad at God because he did not think that God had come through.

If following God is a blessing, then for Jeremiah it was a curse. Nothing seemed to go his way. Wouldn't it be fascinating to have all of our contemporary teachers on prosperity and blessings interact with Jeremiah today? Would Jeremiah believe they were even talking about the same God? Would he have a crisis of faith and wonder if somehow he had missed his calling? Would he have become so embittered toward the God of Israel that he would have recanted his faith and become a follower of the God of America?

I am reminded of a commercial where every person identifies himself as Emmitt Smith. They all claim the same name, but they are not the same person. I think Jeremiah would have faced the same dilemma. We use the name of the same God, but He sure does look different. Jeremiah was following the real God, and what he was experiencing was real life in God. Still ahead of him were attempts on his life, imprisonment, and the indignation of being thrown into a cistern, just to name a few of his upcoming experiences. He would be well prepared to write the poetic literature known as Lamentations.

Jeremiah's life reminds us that even when the beginning point and the final conclusion are certain, the middle can be full of turbulence and instability. Jeremiah's journey began with God's description of His intimate involvement in his life. Before he was formed in the womb, he was known by God. Before he was born, he was set apart, chosen by God for unique and divine purposes. Without even knowing the details, Jeremiah was overwhelmed by God's invitation. His response was one of confessing his own inadequacy and acknowledging his fear. Yet God was unmoved and instructed Jeremiah, "You must go to everyone I send you to and say whatever I command you. Do not be afraid of them, for I am with you and will rescue you" (Jer. 1:7–8).

Not only was his beginning shaped by the finger of God, but he had the promise that in the end he would prevail. He later reinforced that as he unfolded the difficulty of the journey ahead of him. God promised Jeremiah, "They will fight against you but will not overcome you, for I am with you and will rescue you" (Jer. 1:19).

These words from God could be easily understood to mean that every conflict and every difficulty will produce an instantaneous victory and cause for celebration. It is not difficult to see why Jeremiah would feel that God had deceived him. Jeremiah seized his divine moment, but had not fully understood the implications of such a decision. To move with God is not to find the way of escape from the hardships of life. Divine moments are not portals into a world untouched by hardship.

THE CERTAINTY THAT GOD HAS CALLED YOU AND THE CONFIDENCE THAT HE WILL WORK HIS VICTORY OUT IN YOUR LIFE ARE NOT GUARANTEES OF A SAFE AND SECURE JOURNEY.

The certainty that God has called you and the confidence that He will work His victory out in your life are not guarantees of a safe and secure journey. We can draw inspiration from Jeremiah in that he refused to relinquish the gift that God had given him. God had invited him into His purpose to join God on an adventure as a privilege, whatever the cost. Even in his moment of weakness, Jeremiah emerged as a man who must do what was right regardless of consequence. Not all of us are called to Jeremiah's experience, but we are called to his level of commitment.

You need to explore this experience if you are seriously considering engaging this divine journey. If you misunderstand the essence of divine moments, you might find yourself too fainthearted to fully realize God's work in your life. If you're looking for a quick fix out of boredom or hardship, this is not the way. To seize divine moments, you must treasure the invitation to join God. These moments can be fully grasped only when one moment with God is worth to you more than an eternity without Him.

When Jesus told him that in his old age he would be tied and bound and taken to where he did not want to go, Peter responded to this image of his death with a question: "What about John?" I know exactly what he was thinking: I don't mind suffering on Your behalf, Lord, as long as everyone else has to suffer as well. If you were the only one called to suffer, would you still follow?

WHAT'S A MINUTE WORTH?

Several years ago I was faced with this same dilemma. It was early morning and the phone was ringing. My wife, Kim, is a morning person, but I'm quite the opposite. I would only count as a morning person if you factored in that I would often stay up all night until the morning. So when the phone rang before daylight broke, it was a stark and unwanted interruption. It was my little sister, Lei. To the best of my recollection this was the first time she had ever called me. It wasn't that we didn't keep in touch or talk; it was rarely on the phone.

Don't you hate it when someone wakes you up and says, "Are you awake?" You feel obligated to lie. With my sister I fought my way through the grogginess and asked her why she was calling. She hesitated and then asked me a question: "What are you doing today?"

I replied, "Why? What do you mean?"

She asked, "Well, what are you doing today?"

I said, "Nothing in particular that I can think of."

She said, "Well, I had a dream last night. It was about you."

Then I realized that she was weeping on the phone. Now my sister has always been unique, certainly an individual who marches to the beat of a different drummer. When she woke me up to tell me she had a dream about me and began sobbing on the phone, I became a little nervous. I really didn't want to know, but I felt I should ask, "What did you dream?"

She said, "I dreamed that you died." And she repeated it again, "I dreamed that you died today. Are you doing anything dangerous?"

I couldn't think of anything except that I was flying out that night from Dallas to Vegas. It was our denomination's national convention, and I had been invited to speak. After I told her that I was leaving that night, she began to frantically plead with me not to get on that flight. She seemed certain that if I got on the plane, I would be killed. Even for Lei, this conversation was really weird. This is the way bad days start.

A few hours later, I got a phone call from my mother. She began the conversation with a question: "Have you talked to your brother, Alex?"

I said, "No, not recently."

"Do you know if he's okay?" she asked me in somewhat of a panic.

I said, "No, I don't know anything. Why?"

She went on to tell me that she had a dream that one of her two sons was killed. So now my sister had a dream that I died, and my mother had a dream that either I or my brother died. And did I mention I have another sister, who now I am informed had a similar dream? Did I mention I come from a very unusual family?

So I turned to my wife—after all, she has not been affected by the genetic anomaly that has driven all of my family insane. I shared with her all that was going on and told her, "I think my family has lost it."

Kim became very quiet and even pale. She said, "Honey, you know that I never remember my dreams, but two weeks ago I woke up crying in the middle of the night because I dreamed that you had died." Those were not the words of comfort I was looking for from my wife. The whole world around me had gone crazy.

And then there was the weather. We were living in Dallas at the time, and there are these storm formations called Blue Northerns that bring in extreme weather, sometimes snow, sometimes rain. It was one of those kind of days, black clouds, ominous surroundings, lightning that is virtually blinding and thunder that is deafening.

I have to admit the anxiety that the phone calls couldn't fully generate, the weather was able to induce. Kim drove me to the airport that afternoon, a bit nervous that I was leaving under such unusual circumstances. It was pouring down rain when I entered the terminal, which I concluded was a very bad name for an airport building. My flight was delayed: severe weather conditions. There was no certainty when the planes could get off the ground. I began pacing the airport, wondering what was going on. Why was my whole family dreaming that I was going to die? Why were there severe storm conditions on this particular day?

Suddenly I saw a machine over to the side that I had never noticed before. It was one of those instant insurance carriers. You know, the kind you pay your $10 and you get $100,000 of insurance or something like that. I have to admit that I didn't have any life insurance at the time. Never really felt that I needed it. Never really felt that I could die. I was used to flying all the time; it never bothered me. And I know I had never seen one of those insurance machines in my life, not since I began flying at the age of five. So why was it there now? Did they just put it there? Was this the first day that insurance was available at the terminal? Was this God speaking to me, *Erwin, buy insurance; you're going to die today? I felt as if I were already dead.*

I didn't have any cash on me, so I couldn't buy it then. I got some cash with my card, and I went back to the machine. I thought, *This is God giving me an opportunity to take care of my family before He takes me home.* Just as I was placing my money into the mouth of the machine, a different thought ran through my mind: *No, this is God testing me. He's waiting to see if I'm going to put the money into the machine. If I put the money into the machine, He'll know that I don't trust Him, and then He'll kill me. If I don't put the money into the machine, I'll be okay. This is a test of faith.*

I put my money away; I did not purchase the insurance. And for the next hour or so I walked up and down the airport passing by that insurance machine again and again, playing both scenarios in my mind and trying to decide which was the right one. Finally I heard a call for my flight. They had moved our plane to another gate. While the weather was still fierce, they had concluded it was now manageable. I didn't want to get on that plane, and I didn't want to be paralyzed by fear.

As I saw people moving toward the gate, I recognized a famous evangelist in line. I thought, *Maybe he's getting on the plane. God loves him. God would never let him die on this flight.* So I went up to him and asked him if he was getting on the flight to Las Vegas, and he said yes. I felt a little better about getting on the plane. As I boarded the flight, I passed him in first class. Moving on to my seat in coach, I decided what I needed was the comfort of the Scriptures. After I was safely in my seat, tightly buckled, I pulled out my Bible and did what I was always taught in church never to do—I randomly opened it to let God speak to me through Scripture Russian roulette.

Have you ever noticed that if you open your Bible about halfway, it goes to the Minor Prophets? That's exactly what I did. I opened to Amos 4. In a silent whisper I asked God to speak to me from His Word. I looked down, and the first words that came to my line of sight were in verse 12: "Therefore this is what I will do to you . . . and because I will do this to you, prepare to meet your God." It came loud and clear: *Erwin, you are already dead! The event was just a formality.*

It was as if I had been set on fire. All the fear I had suppressed throughout the day came exploding out of my heart into my throat. I heard this loud voice shouting in my head, *We're going to die! We're going to die!* I thought I needed to run to first class and let the man of God know that he needed to pray for us that we would live. And all that kept running through my mind was the phrase "four stupid minutes." I was on this plane for four stupid minutes. I wasn't going to Las Vegas to be a keynote speaker at the Southern Baptist Convention. I had not been invited to fill some prestigious platform role. I had been invited to share for four minutes—that's all, four minutes. You know which four minutes? The four minutes when everyone gets up and goes to the bathroom. The four minutes you go buy your Coke or make the phone call you've been needing to make. Those four minutes. I was going to die for four stupid minutes, and I didn't want to.

It was too late to change my mind. The plane had begun its takeoff. I was determined that as soon as the plane leveled out and the seat belt light went off, I would be in first class pleading my cause. But I had a few minutes until then so I decided to keep reading. Then I came to chapter 5, for God spoke through Amos:

This is what the LORD says to the house of Israel:
Seek me and live;
do not seek Bethel,
do not go to Gilgal,
do not journey to Beersheba.

For Gilgal will surely go into exile,
and Bethel will be reduced to nothing.
Seek the LORD and live. (vv. 4–6)

It was so clear what God was saying to me: *Erwin, seek Me and you will live. Don't run to first class. Don't turn anywhere else. Just seek Me and live.* The question seemed to form in my heart, *Erwin, are you willing to give up everything in order to live four minutes for God?* Of course, at this point, I didn't even know if I was going to get those four minutes, but that wasn't really the point. Was I willing to lose my life trying to do something that was important to God? Would my death, and my life for that matter, find meaning by simply going in the right direction? Was it enough to attempt to do something that would honor God and give Him glory? The answer for me became a resounding yes.

I prayed one prayer in that moment. I asked God to let me have those four minutes to allow me to share what is worth living for and dying for. Not only for the audience who would hear it, but also so that my three-year-old son could one day understand what I considered important in life. I understood in the deepest way of knowing that even if that plane were to crash, I was fully alive. I could not lose the life I had, just a change of residence and an improved body to boot. Is your goal how long you live or that you live? *If you seek Me, you will live, and death will not change that.* After all, when we are in Christ, we have already died in Him, and He has already raised us to a new life.

In that moment the value of each moment became clear to me. I had been willing to live my life for God, but I was keeping the minutes for myself. Yet one moment lived for God is of greater value than an eternity lived without Him. That's the beauty of seeing life through divine moments. It changes not only the content of your life, but also the value of one minute.

I look back on that experience now with the added knowledge that a short time later that evangelist was exposed for his horrifically duplicitous life. He was not what he appeared to be. I was certainly looking in the wrong place for security and reassurance. Life seems to be full of places we can go and hide, places that make us feel safe and secure. For Israel there were places where they had met God, such as Gilgal, Beersheba, and even Bethel. So many places to hide when we should be running to God.

THROUGH THE UNKNOWN DOOR

This is the difference between Jonathan and too many of us. He had no idea whether God would act on his behalf in that particular engagement; he just knew who God was. He knew if he would seek God, he would live, even though he died in the trying. It is ironic that we run to God to keep us safe when He calls us to a dangerous faith. He will shake loose everything in which we place our trust outside of Him and teach us how to thrive in a future unknown. There is only One who is certain; everything else exists in the realm of uncertainty. To place our trust in anything other than God is nothing less than superstition.

> **HE HAD NO IDEA WHETHER GOD WOULD ACT ON HIS BEHALF IN THAT PARTICULAR ENGAGEMENT; HE JUST KNEW WHO GOD WAS.**

Meshach, Shadrach, and Abednego were contemporaries of Daniel. They, too, were selected to serve as advisors to King Nebuchadnezzar. Though they served him well, they infuriated the king when they refused to bow down to the god he had crafted. The king gave them the choice to either bow before his idol or be thrown into a blazing furnace. All three of them chose the fire.

Daniel brought us to the apex of the conflict and recorded his friends' extraordinary response, "O Nebuchadnezzar, we do not need to defend ourselves before you in this matter. If we are thrown into the blazing furnace, the God we serve is able to save us from it, and he will rescue us from your hand, O king. *But even if he does not,* we want you to know, O king, that we will not serve your gods or worship the image of gold you have set up" (Dan. 3:16–18, italics added).

Like Jonathan, the three men knew who God was, and they were confident of what God could do. They also knew they didn't know if He would save them. They understood the uncertainty, but their course of action would be the same in either case. We are told the furnace was then heated seven times hotter. Nebuchadnezzar's strongest soldiers tied the three and then prepared to throw them into the furnace. The fire was so hot it consumed the king's soldiers. Then Shadrach, Meshach, and Abednego fell through the door into the fire.

That was one door I am sure they wished that God had closed rather than left open. I cannot imagine they did not long for God to take them a different way. What must have seemed to them as their last moment would become their greatest moment. The fire did not consume them. A fourth figure met them in the midst of the fire. God met them there. They went to a place they could never go alone and live. God took them on an adventure where not even a king dared journey. When the king invited them to return, they stepped out of the fire. Though they were out of danger, they were more dangerous than ever. The door we fear going through the most may be the very one where we will meet God most profoundly.

I was flying home to Los Angeles on New Year's Eve. I looked beneath me, and a thick layer of clouds made it appear as though there was a gentle cushion, which if necessary would soften any fall. I looked westward and saw the horizon lined with a rich stroke of red and orange, almost accentuating the mystery of what exists beyond our line of sight. I was reflecting on the course of events that had just surrounded the death of Kim's foster father.

Death is one of life's inescapable reminders that we live in a realm of uncertainty. After the memorial the family gathered at Theodore's house. It was late in the evening. Everyone was going home. The family gathering was both unique and peculiar in that all the children were foster children who had received the care of Theodore and Ruth over the years.

HE HAD NO IDEA WHETHER GOD WOULD ACT ON HIS BEHALF IN THAT PARTICULAR ENGAGEMENT; HE JUST KNEW WHO GOD WAS.

As one relative moved toward the door, she asked out loud to herself, "Now which door did I come in from? Was it this one or the other?"

My son, curious about her question, interrupted her and asked, "Why does it matter?"

She responded in a matter-of-fact way, "I always leave from the same place I came."

Curious, Aaron asked, "Why? Are you superstitious?"

She responded, "Yes, about some things I am, and this is one of them."

So Aaron prodded further, "What will happen if you don't go out the door you came in?"

She curtly responded, "I don't know, but I'm not about to find out."

Superstitions have such power to bind and hold us. They also have an unusual ability to let us see into our deepest fears. How many of us feel the compulsion to always go back to where we came from—to return to what we know, to what we can predict, to what we can control? Is it possible that we, too, are afraid to go out a different door? Yes, the new way out is full of uncertainty, but with that uncertainty come mystery, adventure, and wonder. The Jonathan Factor moves you confidently forward into the future when you know that you don't know.

Their sleep was deep but not restful. "Take the flower. With your breath it holds enough for one life. You must decide who among the sleeping will awake."

A fragrance emanated from the earth beneath them, making the air sweet and intoxicating. Its effect was not slumber, but surrender. Most would rather sleep through life than live their dreams.

One would respond to Ayden's breath. To choose wrongly was to waste the healing essence of the iris. If he could only know what dreams held them to their sleep. Maven, if he knew, would offer no clue. Not once did he flinch or change his expression as Ayden moved toward Kembr—face to face, mouth to mouth, then breath to breath.

Her eyes opened and she spoke as if she had known this moment a thousand times before. "Is this yet another dream?"

Ayden questioned her as if she had said nothing: "What dream held you?"

"Only that I had been awakened."

— Entry 828
The Perils of Ayden

4

INFLUENCE

BREATHE IN, BREATHE OUT

STEVE AND JANICE HAVE INVESTED IN CHILDREN FOR years. For over a decade they were the leaders of our centre for child development. Their commitment and unique gifting when it comes to the development of character and potential have always amazed me. So it didn't surprise me when I heard the events that occurred at the children's camp. Out of several hundred children participating in a camp called Adventure Mountain, the seven boys from Mosaic rose to the cream of the crop. With East LA's infamous reputation, to have children from our community selected as the group with the most exemplary behavior was especially sweet. Along with the recognition came reward. It was the coveted right to sleep in the Adventure Mountain tree house.

As their counselor, Steve would have to join them sleeping in the great outdoors. The adventure of sleeping in the tree house could be appropriately entrusted to the best kids in the camp. And there was only one rule that must not be violated: you cannot leave food out. These are real woods with wild animals lurking everywhere. If you are not careful, the scent of food could place you and your campers in serious danger. That should be no problem for the campers who had won for having the cleanest cabin. Besides, the warning of danger should be enough to inspire a handful of nine- and ten-year-olds to take unusual care.

Yet all it took was one boy who heard it not as a warning, but as an opportunity. First he gained the allegiance of a friend and then of the other five. They moved with such care and precision that Steve was entirely unaware of the plot that was brewing. They took potato chips and crushed them and placed them all around the tree house. Along with the chips they sacrificed their much-loved cookies to ensure the success of their plan. Their hopes: to draw out a few raccoons and watch them from the tree house. The result: they were surrounded by raccoons *and* bears. It didn't occur to them that both raccoons *and* bears climb trees.

No one got hurt, but they could have made a deadly mistake. In this case, it just made for an exciting evening. Thank goodness they were the best-behaved kids in the camp. Can you imagine what might have happened if they had let the really bad kids spend a night in the tree house? So the million-dollar question is: How could seven really good kids join together to make such a bad decision? It always begins with one.

Every school has one. Every teacher fears that child. Every parent is certain his child is not the one. You know the one—the corrupting personality, the kid who influences your sweet child to do the wrong thing. That infamous individual who is the cause of every mischievous act from birth to sixth grade. Those children are the notorious influencers of our childhoods. Today, if they're not in prison, they're running Fortune 500 companies, or considering God's love for humor, they're serving somewhere in ministry.

The parental question, *Who put you up to this?* is not really about information gathering. It is an expression of hope. Parents are always hoping someone else put you up to it, that you were not the catalyst of nefarious activity.

For whatever reason, the capacity to influence is usually identified only in the negative during the formative years of our lives. As parents we often wrongly assume that our children will always do good unless influenced toward the bad. The good seems to be reinforced through positional authority and power, otherwise known as Mom and Dad. Without intention, there develops a negative relationship between influence and virtue.

At the same time, as kids we're far more sensitive and attracted to the magnetic force of peer influence than we are of parental authority. And frankly I don't think this ever changes. We are always more open to influence than we are to authority. We would much rather be magnetically pulled in a direction than controlled by the force of power and consequence.

Human beings are created with the capacity to influence and be influenced. This is inherent in that we are created as relational beings. It is heightened by the reality that we are not simply intellectual but emotional creatures. Influence can be a great thing, especially when we distinguish it from manipulation.

INFLUENCE IS THE BEST WAY TO LEAD AND MOVE OTHERS TOWARD WHAT IS GOOD.

Manipulation is the use of influence to control others for personal gain. It is the dark side of influence. Manipulation could be described as a relational lie. It is not merely deception in language, but the corruption of trust. When we manipulate, we deceive those who trust not only our words, but also our intent. All of us have the capacity to manipulate and must guard ourselves from violating relationships at this level. Yet at the same time, we must not confuse manipulation with influence.

While manipulation is inherently evil, influence is the best way to lead and move others toward what is good. The proper use of influence is essential if we are going to seize divine moments. We must always remember that God's greatest moments for us are never for us alone. They are always about our lives touching the lives of others. For too long we have accepted the popular notion of a faith that is just for us. This is nothing more than the spiritu-alization of a life that is just about me—a life of selfishness. There is a difference between a private faith and a personal faith. Though God meets us as unique individuals, His intention is never an individualis-tic faith. A life touched by God always ends in touching others.

A LIFE TOUCHED BY GOD ALWAYS ENDS IN TOUCHING OTHERS.

THE **FLIP SIDE** OF **INFLUENCE**

In my experience one of the places we feel most powerless is our abil-ity to bring positive influence to the world around us. We see so many things that need to be fixed, so many things that could be improved, but no one will seem to listen to our ideas. This is espe-cially true in the workplace. I can't begin to count how many times I've heard employees complain about their work situation. Whatever the vocation or environment, the problem is always the same: it's their boss. The scenario is pretty consistent. Their boss doesn't have a clue and won't listen.

It is amazing how many companies have the person with all the right answers working for the person who doesn't even know the questions. As you can imagine, the solution is always the same: "Fire my boss and give me his job." This is the solution to almost every workplace conflict I've ever encountered—if I accept the analysis of disgruntled employees.

It's no different in the church. In my years of consulting work with these nonprofit communities of faith, I'm amazed at the level of frustration that I've encountered. It almost always comes down to influence. Someone wants to bring change, whether it's seismic or incremental. He feels frustrated in his attempts. Someone with more authority than he has refuses to consider his idea, will not hear him out, or just doesn't get it.

The same would be true in any organization when you're the new kid on the block or the low man on the totem pole. You see things a new way. You have fresh eyes. You're inspired, enthusiastic, and ready to go, but no one will listen to you. You wonder why they even bothered to hire you if they didn't value your contribution. No one seems to recognize your potential. They could have hired a monkey to do what you do. In the meantime, you waste your hours away wishing you could make a difference.

Marriage can be that way too. For generations men have been given carte blanche to rule the home from the position of power and authority. Not only children, but wives have felt powerless to have any real role in shaping the texture of the family. Our society has often been deaf to the cries of women who feel powerless to shape their lives. At the same time, feminism has empowered women to pursue the same instruments of power that once held them oppressed. The solution to the sense of powerlessness, the solution to ending the unethical use of power by men, is to seize the same power and influence and use them the same way. Nothing has changed at the core. No genuine shift in value systems. It's just more crowded at the top with everyone pushing each other off as we lust for more power, more authority, more position.

We have lost confidence in the power of influence, and because of that, we have lost the beauty of its art. The problem with positional power is that while it may control the actions of another human being, it does not capture the heart. God

> **WE HAVE LOST CONFIDENCE IN THE POWER OF INFLUENCE, AND BECAUSE OF THAT, WE HAVE LOST THE BEAUTY OF ITS ART. THE PROBLEM WITH POSITIONAL POWER IS THAT WHILE IT MAY CONTROL THE ACTIONS OF ANOTHER HUMAN BEING, IT DOES NOT CAPTURE THE HEART.**

is looking for women and men who will be characterized by this Jonathan Factor, who understand, develop, and maximize their sphere of influence.

I AM WITH YOU

Samuel told us, "No one was aware that Jonathan had left . . . Jonathan said to his young armor-bearer, 'Come, let's go over to the outpost of those uncircumcised fellows. Perhaps the LORD will act in our behalf. None can hinder the LORD from saving, whether by many or by few.'"

Samuel then recorded the response of Jonathan's armor-bearer: "Do all that you have in mind. Go ahead; I am with you heart and soul."

Jonathan had a keen sense of his sphere of influence. It is as important to note what he did not do as to take notice of what he did do. Jonathan did not wake up his father, Saul. He understood that his father, as king, had already made up his mind. He was not going to attack the Philistines; he was going to stay under the pomegranate tree. That conversation was over. Jonathan could neither force nor convince Saul to change his mind. It was irrelevant whether he approached him as king or as father. Saul remained unmoved.

Many times we conclude we are powerless because we cannot change things "up." Those who hold positions of power and authority simply will not see things our way. All too often when we cannot change things up, we conclude that we cannot change anything.

If Jonathan accepted this paradigm of powerlessness, he would have never seized his divine moment. At the same time, he did not attempt to persuade the six hundred men who were under Saul's leadership. Jonathan was not inciting an insurrection. He did not consider turning the soldiers of King Saul into the warriors of Prince Jonathan. He understood he had not been given authority over the army, and he did not cross that boundary.

How many times have we concluded we were powerless to make a difference because the available resources were withheld from us? Jonathan could have easily concluded that since he could not rightfully access the warriors, he was powerless to do anything. There is an implicit conversation hidden in this text. It is highly unlikely that Jonathan would not have first attempted to persuade his father to attack the Philistines. That he had to sneak out in the night tells us that Jonathan knew his father would be against his action. I can only imagine that the conversation between a young warrior and the elder king was similar to many conversations still being held today. How many young, emerging leaders have been frustrated when those over them no longer demonstrate the level of urgency that moved them to their places of authority? How many times have those in leadership abdicated their responsibility to lead simply to hold on to what they have? Saul was paralyzed because he had too much to lose. And history shows us that Saul's unwillingness to trust God cost him everything in the end. When Jonathan left in the middle of the night, waking no one except his armor-bearer, it is clear that Saul would neither go nor entrust his resources to Jonathan.

HOW MANY TIMES HAVE WE CONCLUDED WE WERE POWERLESS TO MAKE A DIFFERENCE BECAUSE THE AVAILABLE RESOURCES WERE WITHHELD FROM US?

Two roadblocks that often mislead us are lack of authority and lack of resources. Jonathan would have been totally justified in choosing to do nothing. He could have easily been paralyzed by the conditions he faced. He could have even accepted them as undeniable signs that God did not want him to advance. After all, what can one person really do?

There's much to learn from Jonathan's next action. He didn't attempt to override the king who had rightful authority, he didn't attempt to steal or take what was not his, but he didn't allow his limitations to limit him. Saul had given him one sword, and it was his right to use it. He had placed under his authority one person, and he called him out to follow him, and even in that relationship Jonathan was an inspiration. Jonathan was not acting under military command and thus did not attempt to command even his armor-bearer to follow him. He simply invited him. Jonathan knew that there was more than a relationship of authority between him and the young man, that he had invested into his apprentice's life and had gained his allegiance.

As a servant, the young man was required to obey his master. But the armor-bearer expressed more than obedience; he expressed his allegiance. That Jonathan was initiating without the king's approval would have been clear to the armor-bearer. Even the slightest misstep would have awakened Saul and his men. Jonathan's servant could have easily sabotaged his master's intention. He

TITLE, POSITION, AND AUTHORITY MAY HOLD POWER, BUT INFLUENCE TRAVELS THROUGH RELATIONSHIPS. AND IN THE END, INFLUENCE IS THE FOUNTAINHEAD OF POWER.

would have been justified to reject Jonathan's request out of loyalty to the king. What we find is a deeper loyalty. Not simply loyalty to nation or king, or loyalty to the son of a king, but loyalty to a man—Jonathan. Title, position, and authority may hold power, but influence travels through relationships. And in the end, influence is the fountainhead of power.

The armor-bearer's response unlocked the power of influence:

"Do all that you have in mind. Go ahead; I am with you heart and soul." This is the essence of influence, to win the heart and soul of another person through the strength of your own character and personhood. This is why influence is always more powerful than authority. Authority can shape what a person does, but influence shapes who a person becomes. Influence is born out of trust and finds its strength in the connection of heart and soul. Like Jonathan, we must step into the full extent of our appropriate influence if we are to seize divine moments. We must not be afraid to call those who would listen to follow into an uncertain future. Spiritual influence is not only a gift; it is a responsibility. What Jonathan would find is that while his initial influence was limited, his commitment to do what was right, to seize this divine moment, would expand his sphere of influence to an unexpected level.

INFLUENCE IS CONTAGIOUS

First my mom caught it, then she passed it to my sister. We're not really sure which one of the two more directly gave it to my brother, but then between the three of them, my other sister got it too. So I found myself living in a house with what I considered some really sick people. I did everything I could to avoid being infected. Have you ever been around a bunch of people with the flu, or more specifically, influenza?

Well, this was no different for me. They had it really bad, and they were terribly contagious. They had all become Christians, and they were determined to infect everyone around them. Maybe you've been there. If you're there right now, be warned: Christians are very contagious.

Have you ever looked at the middle of the word *influence?* What do you see? It's hidden right there. *F-l-u.* That's right, the flu. People who are influential pass on what they have like the flu.

If you don't want what they've got, stay away from them because they'll sneeze all over you. You may not even see it happen. Those aggressive, invisible germs passing from one person to another—there's no escaping them.

Influence is contagious, and if you want to know how influence works, just follow the trail of influenza. It is airborne and passes most quickly through human contact, but proximity still endangers your contamination. And like the common cold, some things have no vaccines and no cures. You can't see them pass from one person to another, but you know when they have you. And we are all carriers—not of a dangerous virus, I hope, but carriers of character. And through our character, we pass on attitudes, values, and other life-shaping virtues. All of us pass a bit of ourselves on to others. You better like who you are and make what you give to others from yourself a gift and not a curse.

ALL OF US PASS A BIT OF OURSELVES ONTO OTHERS. YOU BETTER LIKE WHO YOU ARE AND MAKE WHAT YOU GIVE TO OTHERS FROM YOURSELF A GIFT AND NOT A CURSE.

Kim and I see a lot of ourselves in our kids; we just disagree which part they got from her and which part they got from me. But there's no denying that we've sneezed on them, and they've been infected by who we are. A few years ago, Kim had volunteered on Mother's Day to work with the eight-year-old class on Sunday morning. She was helping all the children put together special Mother's Day cards that they could hand to their moms as soon as they came out of church.

Our daughter, Mariah, was in Kim's class that morning, and she seemed to have a mental block about the project. Kim felt funny about it, but knew she needed to help her create her own Mother's Day card. She explained again to Mariah that she needed to write on the card what she felt about her mother, and Mariah's answer was, "You mean my daddy?" She said, "No, you need to write down how you feel about your mommy." She said, "No, you mean my daddy." Kim explained that Mariah cried in the car all the way home, saying, "I wanted to talk about my daddy today in class, and you wouldn't let me." I love this story.

There's something very special about having a daddy's girl, but it reminds me of the immense responsibility we all have as fathers due to the influence in our children's lives. Of course, we know the same is true for moms, but it's also true for children, for employers, for employees, for all of us. We are all contagious. Let's make sure that we infect people with the right things.

Character is the resource from which influence draws. Relationships are the venue through which influence travels. **More often than not, God's invitation to us to seize divine moments is found in the needs of other people's lives.** To fully live each day, we must recognize the centrality of relationships. James told us that the royal law of Scripture is to love your neighbor as yourself. Jesus attached this call to relational living to His command that we love God with all of our being. When you summarize the Great Commandment with one word, it would be relationships. Nothing matters to God more than relationships. They are the source and context for eternal life. Having a right relationship with God results in having right relationships with others. The investment, and thus the influence in the lives of others, is one of the most significant ingredients of a person who seizes divine moments.

YOU NEVER KNOW WHOM YOU TOUCH

Influence is defined as "a power affecting a person, thing, or course of events"—especially one that operates without any direct or apparent effort. Most of us have yet to comprehend our capacity to influence others in a positive way. We just do not see how far our influence can travel. We underestimate how deeply our influence can change a person's life. And there is no way to fully measure how many people our influence will affect when it runs its course. We can get a clearer sense of the flow of influence when we remember that influence flows through relationships and that relationships begin at the first point of contact.

Dave was a UPS driver for thirteen years. The nature of his job required him to interact with an endless number of people, but he wasn't really able to spend much time with them. He had to engage as many people as possible per day while moving on as quickly as he could. Anything that slowed him down jeopardized both his effectiveness and his employment. Though he interacted with hundreds of people a day, the relationships were never more than superficial. That was not because Dave valued superficial relationships, but because his job demanded them.

Dave's encounters with other people on his route in Los Angeles might be described as drive-by relationships. But in spite of these conditions, Dave discovered that his influence in the life of at least one person was more profound than he could have ever imagined. Dave tells it like this:

"Ron was one of those stream-of-consciousness communicators. He was a gas station attendant in Santa Monica on my route. I have to admit I dreaded anytime I had to deliver a package anywhere near the corner of Twentieth and Santa Monica Boulevard. That's where Ron's gas station was located.

"If my package car was parked within a half-block radius of that intersection, Ron would somehow find me. He would talk to me while I was in the cab, writing up packages, loading them onto my handcart as I walked to the offices. He would follow me as other people would sign for their packages and talk to me as I returned to my truck, loaded my handcart and started my engine, and wouldn't stop until I was actually rolling away from him. Now don't get me wrong, Ron was a nice guy, but he definitely put a crimp in my day.

"One afternoon Ron was somewhat less verbal, and I thought something was up. Before I actually left in my truck, he handed me a small white envelope. I asked him if he wanted me to open it right there, and he said, 'Yeah.' So I obliged, and it turned out to be an invitation to a wedding. Ron was planning on marrying a young woman named Joanne, and he wanted to invite me, the local UPS driver, to his wedding. I politely thanked him for the invitation and purposefully avoided answering him on the spot.

"For the next three weeks the only thing Ron ever wanted to talk to me about was whether or not I was planning to come to the wedding. This not only slowed down my day, but it also became excruciatingly painful to find creative ways to avoid answering. I finally checked my calendar for the date and realized that there was a leadership meeting planned for the same time as Ron's wedding. Being the dedicated, faithful Christian leader I am, I realized that unfortunately I wasn't going to be able to make it to Ron and Joanne's nuptials.

"As I pulled up to the alley behind the gas station, I knew Ron would be there waiting for me, and I had my answer prepared: 'Thank you for the invitation, but I have a prior commitment. Be sure to send my best to your new bride.' Sure enough, as I opened the back of my package car, Ron was standing there waiting, as usual.

"And he asked me, 'Are you going to come to the wedding next week?' And I don't know what happened. In every fiber of my being a 'no' was forming. But as I opened my mouth I said, 'Yes, of course I'm coming to your wedding.'

"Ron's face lit up like a Roman candle, and he said, 'Great. Looking forward to seeing you.' And he ran back to his gas station. I stood there for a few seconds petrified, not believing what I had just committed to and trying to figure out how I was going to explain to my wife that I wouldn't be going to our leadership meeting.

"Saturday morning came faster than I had anticipated. I woke up and dressed in my proper wedding attire, and I realized that I had failed to pick up a card or gift for Ron and Joanne's wedding. I grabbed my video camera and a blank tape and figured I would videotape something at the wedding or at the reception and give it to them as a stand-in gift. I arrived at the wedding about half an hour early, came into the lobby, and was greeted by an usher who asked politely, 'Bride or groom?'

"I said, 'Groom,' and he escorted me into the small church and offered me a seat on the right side. I slid across the pew to the wall, plugged in my video camera and set up my tripod, took my time, and waited for the rest of the guests to arrive. People trickled into the church, and row by row, the left side of the church was filling. No seats in front of me on the right side had anyone occupying them. About five minutes before the wedding was to begin, twenty to twenty-five people from the left side of the church stood up, walked across the aisle, and sat on the right side of the auditorium.

"The wedding march rang from the organ, the bride walked down the aisle, and the groom greeted her. They exchanged their vows and exited the church, all smiles. I broke down the camera equipment and headed to my car, planning on handing off the videotape and leaving. Ron saw me heading to my car and followed me and asked, 'You're coming to the reception, aren't you?' To which I sheepishly replied, 'Of course. I'm just dropping off my equipment.' He said, 'Great, I'll see you there.'

"Now I was committed to another two hours of getting to know people whom I would probably never see again. I drove to the reception, which was in the backyard of one of the parents' homes. There was a long table set out on the grass with the wedding party surrounding it and several guests milling around and eating reception goodies. I grabbed my video camera and decided I would try to record just some casual comments of wedding guests.

"While I was videotaping the reception, different people rose to give toasts and say thanks. Eventually Ron, the groom, stood. Looking straight back at the camera, Ron professed his eternal love for his beautiful bride and his dreams of their life together. And then to all present, he said he wanted to thank his best friend for being a part of the wedding that day. As I moved in for the close-up, Ron said, 'I'd like you to meet my best friend, Dave.'

"As every head in the yard turned around to look at the guy standing in the back with the camera, it suddenly hit me: Ron saw me as someone very important in his life. And I saw Ron as someone who slowed down my day, someone whose wedding I begrudgingly agreed to attend. After Ron made his comments and the reception began breaking up, he came back and gave me a big hug and told me news that further caused me to realize how important my coming was to Ron. He thanked me for coming and then told me he had sent out more than 150 invitations—invitations to his friends from the gas station, to his family, to his neighbors. And of all the people he had personally invited, I was the only one who attended the wedding."

What Dave perceived to be a stranger's invitation to his wedding was actually God's invitation to seize a divine moment. Dave's presence, though reluctant, became God's venue for reaching into Ron's life. Dave became a significant voice in Ron and Joanne's future marriage and became the guide who brought Ron into a faith with the God who loves him. Dave's influence in their lives was as significant as it was surprising. The power of influence when we seize divine moments can be disproportionate to its apparent importance. What may look like an inconvenience might be no less than the beginning of a life-changing opportunity.

Often divine moments look like inconveniences on the front end. It is virtually impossible to predict the range or depth of impact that can result in the lives of others when we seize these God-given opportunities. Our sphere

OFTEN DIVINE MOMENTS LOOK LIKE INCONVENIENCES ON THE FRONT END.

of influence is no small part in this journey. We must never underestimate where influence can take us.

One of the ways we miss divine moments is to treat what we consider nominal influence as irrelevant. We must never underestimate the importance of one moment, one word, one deed in the life of another human being.

YOUR TOUCH MAY BE FAR-REACHING

As Jonathan's story progresses, we discover that his influence would go much farther than to his armor-bearer. What seemed at first a very limited scope of influence, in the end, found an unlimited range of impact. While he never had authority over his father, his decision to seize his divine moment resulted in influence over the king of Israel. As we will find as the story develops, Jonathan's initiative, which began with very little influence, would influence his father, the king, to join him in the battle. Divine opportunities are sometimes like windows, but other times they are like corridors. You have to walk through them and keep walking before you get to the other side.

Dolores Kube began working in south Dallas as a summer missionary. She had a deep and passionate commitment to working with underprivileged children. She later became a permanent feature in the lives of many in south Dallas. For the next twenty years she would serve as the local missionary through the Ervay Baptist Center. Dolores became a personal friend to Kim and me and was a continuous source of inspiration. She would drive through the neighborhood in her small Toyota and pack it with children so they could join her Bible clubs. She was a friend and confidante to many single moms and fatherless children. She was essentially the Mother Teresa of south Dallas. It never surprised me when the children would refer to Cornerstone as Mrs. Kube's church.

Then one day, through arson, the center was burned to the ground. For most it was more than the destruction of a building; it was the end of a dream. The mission organization that financed the center withdrew its support and closed the chapter on the work. Like all the other evangelical churches, they, too, were giving up on the impoverished community. The endless amount of resources poured into the community had at best a nominal impact. The lack of return on investment was once again the death sentence of another urban ministry. Yet Dolores and a handful of others used a different scale of measure. They believed in what God was doing in south Dallas. And though perhaps a product of their efforts remained intangible, they were committed to the cause.

With the close of the center came the end of her salary and the end of her appointment as a missionary; however, she refused to leave. Her sheer tenacity rallied others around her and built a support base for her work. It was because she did not quit that I found myself in south Dallas in 1983. There were less than a dozen adults who made up the core of the remnant ministry. They had struggled through about a half dozen pastors who attempted to restart the work. Without Dolores's commitment, I would have never become the leader of a small but committed team of people that one day would become Cornerstone.

For the next six years I had the privilege of partnering with Dolores as we watched this handful of people flourish into a thriving spiritual community. At the end of those six years, I led Cornerstone to accept my resignation and call a young African-American man to become the new pastor. Chris Simmons had begun as an intern, then became an associate pastor, then served as copastor, and in the end would become the senior pastor of Cornerstone. He has served in that position for the past fourteen years.

During our transition the elder George Bush was president of the United States, and he appointed William Bennett as the drug czar. He was on a national search for solutions to America's drug problem. He would visit city after city to both encourage and validate the best work in this arena. When he came to Dallas, the city officials were asked to recommend a reference point of effectiveness in the war on drugs. The city of Dallas sent him to Cornerstone. His day in Dallas was hosted out of Cornerstone's facility in this small church in an impoverished community. This is more astonishing when you consider that on our best Easter, we probably did not have more than two hundred adults in attendance. Who could have ever projected that Dolores's work in a small duplex with a handful of children whose families were on welfare would result twenty years later in this kind of recognition and influence?

Remember that influence is a power affecting a person, thing, or course of events. Many times the events that we would describe as having significant importance or impact can be traced back to the humble influence

ONE OF THE TRAGEDIES OF NEGLECTING GOD-GIVEN OPPORTUNITIES IS THAT WE ARE NEVER AWARE OF THE BREADTH OF INFLUENCE AND OUTCOME THAT WE HAVE MISSED.

of a person who was never recognized publicly. One of the tragedies of neglecting God-given opportunities is that we are never aware of the breadth of influence and outcome that we have missed. Jonathan's personal act of courage resulted in a national triumph. Never underestimate how far God can take the momentum of what you feel is your nominal influence.

REAL INFLUENCE GOES DEEP

Influence can do what command can never do; it can win the hearts of people. You can pay people to do a job, but you can't pay them to change their minds or, more accurately, to change their hearts. External power has the limitation of bringing external change. Influence is the material of internal power. Again, influence is not about position or delegated authority or endless forms of power. Influence is born out of a person, who that person is, and translates to how it affects the heart of another person. Real influence goes deep. It changes how a person feels about something. It has direct impact not only on how a person acts, but also on what he believes and what he is committed to.

We understand the difference between authority and influence when we watch our children grow up. What your children act like when they're under your authority is very different from who they become as a result of your influence. Many parents become brokenhearted when they realize that their influence on their children is at best minimal, at worst inconsequential, compared to the influence of others in their lives. I am convinced that great parenting is all about influence. It is more about shaping values than it is about setting boundaries.

Jonathan's armor-bearer expressed a level of loyalty that is rarely found in our time. He said, "I am with you heart and soul." It was not about obligation. He was not acting out of compliance.

It wasn't that he understood everything Jonathan was going to do or even agreed with Jonathan's approach or strategy. It wasn't Jonathan's idea that he was agreeing with. He believed in Jonathan. He trusted who Jonathan was. He said, "Do all that you have in mind," and then declared that he was with him.

As a parent, I've discovered that the love and respect my children have for me are far more powerful than any rules or potential punishment. I've also found that there's no more rewarding experience than when my children are motivated by their own value systems to do what is right. It is without question that value systems are transferred through a connection of the heart. Even though my kids have grown up in church, their love for truth is not the result of exhaustive research. Their desire to do good is not the result of logical deduction. Their values have been passed on through genuine relationship and trust. And one thing I am eternally grateful for is that we pass on not just who we are, but who we genuinely desire to become. Our children see our flaws, our faults, and yes, even our sins. The compensating grace is that they are also able, when we in humility repent and confess our shortcomings, to see what we aspire to be. Our influence is not limited to our present condition. It is expanded by our intended destination when we are committed to the journey. Influence is rooted in character—who we are and who we are becoming. Influence transfers best and moves most quickly whenever respect and trust are present. When the environment is right, influence goes deep. It goes to the very core of who we are.

OUR INFLUENCE IS NOT LIMITED TO OUR PRESENT CONDITION. IT IS EXPANDED BY OUR INTENDED DESTINATION WHEN WE ARE COMMITTED TO THE JOURNEY.

The most important influences in people's lives are the ones who have helped shape who they are. You really can know a person by his friends. Trustworthy people are surrounded by people who trust them. And women and men who are genuinely Christlike are surrounded by those who long to be more like Christ. Character breeds influence. Influence shapes character. The relationship between character and influence is like breathing—the deeper you inhale, the stronger you can exhale. Take your character deep, and your influence will be profound.

A GIFT INTENDED FOR GOOD

Unfortunately this works in two dramatic directions. Character does breed influence. Whether it is godly character or ungodly character, the principle still applies. Hitler was a person of tremendous influence. Certainly few would describe his character as virtuous, yet he won the heart and soul of a nation. The same would be true for Stalin, for Mao, and for many others. History teaches us that those who are committed to nobility or to evil become the sources of tremendous influence. Recognizing this should only heighten our urgency and our sense of responsibility.

Again, we as human beings are relational creatures. We are all influential. We can influence others and are influenced by others. If only those who are committed to evil set out to influence the many, then we should not be surprised that there is very little good in the world. A significant part of seizing divine moments is recognizing that God's intention is to use us as vessels for good. Not simply to do good, but to generate good, to

A SIGNIFICANT PART OF SEIZING DIVINE MOMENTS IS RECOGNIZING THAT GOD'S INTENTION IS TO USE US AS VESSELS FOR GOOD. NOT SIMPLY TO DO GOOD, BUT TO GENERATE GOOD, TO LEAD OTHERS TOWARD GOOD.

lead others toward good. This is nothing less than a battle for the hearts of people. Certainly few things are more rewarding than being a positive influence in the life of another human being.

Myra was four years old when I met her. Her mother, Rosa, lived her life in a wheelchair. When she was a child, a sickness had cost her both legs. My first memory of Myra was of three women trying to catch her when she refused to come to her mother. It was an absolutely hilarious scene that I almost hated bringing to an end. Myra was bright, fast, and elusive. And with all their chasing and her mother's urgent commands, Myra was not going to be caught. I volunteered to intervene, but I was determined not to chase Myra. I knelt quite a distance from her, and I spoke to her in Spanish, which was the only language she understood. I explained to her that I was faster than she was and that the moment I chose to I, unlike the others chasing her, would catch her immediately. But I would give her another option. She could come to me of her own will, and I would make sure that all was forgiven. I could almost feel her thinking as she considered her options. Then she very quietly walked to me, and a new friendship was born.

Myra and her mother came to live with Kim and me for nearly a year. Myra's first night was filled with testing the limits and strong emotions. When she began to speak to her mother with disrespect, I explained to her that she would not speak to her mother that way in our home. Myra looked at me with her little brown eyes and told me she was going to call her grandfather in Mexico and have me killed. We had a long way to go, a lot of pain to work through, a lot of anger and hate to replace with love and acceptance. It didn't take very long. The human heart was designed for love. The changes that we saw and experienced in Myra's heart were not just a gift to her, but also a gift to us. There may be no greater reward than to experience the life change of another human being through the investment of your influence. But to have this kind of influence, you have to let people come close.

Victor is a giant of a Puerto Rican. He would be physically intimidating, if not for his inviting warmth and jovial personality, always smiling and filled with unending enthusiasm. He had been a follower of Christ for less than a year, but he was the obvious choice to take my place as pastor of El Pueblo de Dios. Needing to place him in a context for accelerated spiritual growth, I invited him to live with us in our home. He seemed both surprised and apprehensive when I extended our invitation. He later explained to me that his hesitation was that I would be his spiritual leader, and if he lived with us, I would see him in his underwear. In his own unique way, Victor was telling me, "I'm not sure if I'm ready for that level of investment." Was it safe to live in a relationship where he'd be so exposed? After all, can you afford to let your boss see your dirty laundry? In spite of all his apprehensions, Victor chose to come.

Before he did, I reminded him of one important factor: I was inviting him to observe us up close. We, too, would not be able to hide who we are. This was not a formal discipleship structure. It was an invitation to enter

THE ULTIMATE END AND MOST PROFOUND RESULT OF INFLUENCE IS WHEN A PERSON IS FREE FROM ANY COMMAND OR POWER YOU MAY EXERT AND YET STILL REFLECTS THE INFLUENCE OF YOUR VALUES AND PASSIONS.

our lives and know us for who we really are. It didn't take a year before Victor replaced me as pastor of El Pueblo de Dios. If you want to increase your influence, risk bringing people up close. Of course, it is important to first ask yourself the question, *If I bring someone close enough to see the real me, what will he see? Who will he become?*

DIVINE INFLUENCE

The ultimate end and most profound result of influence is when a person is free from any command or power you may exert and yet still reflects the influence of your values and passions. That being said, it becomes more profound when we begin to consider the influence of Jesus. His life two thousand years ago continues to shape the hearts and souls of millions around the world—not motivated by the fear of judgment or the uncertainty of salvation, but in fact promised through the grace of God's irrevocable relationship. After all, once you promise a person forgiveness, once you guarantee a relationship built on unconditional love, what are you left with to force a person to do your will? Isn't this God's dilemma? No coercion, no threat of rejection—freedom from punishment, judgment, and rejection. What motivates a Christian now?

Jesus Christ is the greatest example of true influence reaching into the heart and soul of a person, changing him from the inside out. When God does it, it's the miraculous work of transformation. Yet in the end, it is still rooted in influence. God wins our hearts. We move with Him because He has earned our trust, and we long to be at His side. This is the model that Jonathan reinforces. This is the challenge that is set before us—that we not only take initiative, that we not only move with confidence into the reality of uncertainty, but also that we maximize our sphere of influence as we grow in depth of character.

THIS IS THE CHALLENGE THAT IS SET BEFORE US—THAT WE NOT ONLY TAKE INITIATIVE, THAT WE NOT ONLY MOVE WITH CONFIDENCE INTO THE REALITY OF UNCERTAINTY, BUT ALSO THAT WE MAXIMIZE OUR SPHERE OF INFLUENCE AS WE GROW IN DEPTH OF CHARACTER.

"You must leave while it is still night," Maven reminded Ayden.

"Is that so we might slip past the shadows before they wake?" Kembr asked hopefully.

"No!" snapped Ayden. "It is so they know that it was we who woke them and dared interrupt their sleep!"

"The way is full of peril. Must we beckon it?" asked Kembr.

Maven knew it was not fear but thought that guided Kembr's queries. He looked past Ayden and spoke to her what she already knew from her dreams.

"The shadows rule the night. They hide blinded by the day and thus cannot be seen. The day is free. It is during the night they take mankind captive, keeping them in their slumber."

Ayden continued Maven's thoughts, "We must walk into the shadow's darkest place. Only there will we know if we have light enough."

— Entry 988
The Perils of Ayden

5

RISK

LIVE BEFORE YOU DIE, AND VICE VERSA

I GOT A MESSAGE THROUGH THE URBAN GRAPEVINE that I was dead. It might surprise you that in the dark corridors of the urban jungle there are many prophets—mostly prophets of doom. This angel of death went by the name William. Through my work in one of the projects, his common-law wife had come to a personal faith in Jesus Christ. He was in prison and heard the news of her conversion. He did not consider this good news. I had trespassed onto his territory. A crime punishable—yes, that's right, you got it—by death. So I got the word—several times actually—that when he got out of prison, I was going to be his first stop. He had spent most of his adult life behind prison walls, and by his own description, he had broken all of the commandments. This time he had gone to prison for slitting a man's throat. That man was the brother of his common-law wife, whom we will call Lupe.

When I heard he was released from prison, I decided to find him before he found me. He lived in a small apartment complex surrounded mostly by dilapidated houses and run-down store-fronts. The complex was walking distance from the skyscrapers downtown and sat in the middle of what had once been one of the city's most prestigious neighborhoods. You don't ever forget meeting someone like William. He was in some ways an ethnic anomaly. He was a white guy in the middle of a Latin community who had a reputation for being good with a knife. He was in his mid-thirties, and life had made him as hard as stone.

We sat face-to-face in a dingy apartment filled with loud children and usually inebriated neighbors. But before I knew it, we were there alone—just William and me. I don't recall how it happened. I never noticed the exodus. It was only the silence and discomfort of the moment that made me aware of how everything had changed. Metal bars on the windows, the door soundly shut. We were alone.

He swiftly reached into his jacket, pulled out a knife, and with a quick move of his wrist opened it where its position made the metal gleam in my direction. Like someone remembering a secret pleasure, he smiled and said, "This is the knife I slit his throat with. The police never got it."

A thousand thoughts were rushing through my mind. But I really didn't have any material in the category of "witty responses to use shortly before dying at knifepoint." I remember entertaining the thought that Lupe's brother didn't die; William just cut off his vocal cords. That thought was not at all comforting. I knew my next, my first, perhaps my last sentence was of utmost importance. And then the words came. It was as if I heard them for the first time even as he heard them.

"William, that knife is going to send you to hell!" I looked straight into his eyes, and I knew he was shocked that I said it. To be really honest, I was shocked that I said it. But I was still breathing, which allowed me to gain courage. And so I proceeded: "You think you're tough—" Halfway through my sentence I heard a scream in my head, *What are you thinking?* So I adjusted. "Well, William, you are tough, but you're not free. You're not in prison, but you're still a prisoner. Behind every shadow there's someone waiting to kill you."

Somehow William's normal approach to life, one of violence and retaliation, was restrained that day. He listened, and we established a strange kind of friendship. I wish I could tell you that William's life changed that day or that it changed some other day in the future, but best I can tell, William's life never changed. But what did happen I'll never forget. William became my John the Baptist, who would prepare the way for me throughout the streets of south Dallas. He often boasted that he and I were friends because, as he would put it, he was radical for evil and I was radical for God.

PASSING TO THE OTHER SIDE

William and I had met on the other side of a divine moment. To use the language of Jonathan's experience, we had crossed over; we had walked through the pass. When Jonathan spoke to his armor-bearer and convinced him to go with him to engage the Philistines, not only did he acknowledge his uncertainty of whether God would actually help them, but he then laid out a dangerous strategy that made him look as if he were out of his mind. You might have already concluded that, but this will only confirm it.

Jonathan said, "Come, then; we will cross over toward the men and let them see us." Now I'm not a military expert. I've never been to West Point. I have never even been a Boy Scout. But I think I know enough to realize this is a terrible military strategy.

Let them see us? Don't you mean, *Let's sneak up on them, hide in the shadows, maintain radio silence, and attack through stealth strikes?* This particular approach just doesn't make any sense. When you're out-manned, outnumbered, outequipped, you don't just come out. Their only hope would be to remain virtually invisible.

Yet Jonathan somehow knew that this particular engagement was not a matter of human ingenuity. He was moving out to seize a divine moment. It wasn't a moment he was simply going to create, though it would not come without his initiative. He was stepping into a moment where God would have to come through if it was going to achieve its ultimate end. He was not being presumptuous about God. He clearly knew who God was and also understood the potential consequence of his action. He was, in a very real sense, creating an opportunity for God to bring the victory He had already promised.

REMOVING THE CLOAK OF INVISIBILITY

The story went on: "So both of them showed themselves to the Philistine outpost." There is something about divine moments that requires us to go through the pass, to venture beyond the point of no return. Divine moments require us to move from the invisible to the visible so that the invisible can become visible.

Many of us live our lives making sure we are not seen. We choose the cloak of invisibility. We call it by another name, but the result is the same. We choose to remain anonymous. We treasure our anonymity. We choose to remain uninvolved, and our love for personal privacy disguises both our indifference and our isolation. You can live your life and never be seen. Yes, the opposite ambition has potential for huge problems. Just as remaining invisible can be motivated by a refusal to get involved, becoming visible can be motivated by craving to be the center of attention. But I'm not talking about inappropriately seeking the limelight. This is not about making life a stage and demanding the starring role. This is about stepping up and making sure your life counts. It's about volunteering when God is asking, "Who will go on My behalf?" I'm talking about our silent abdication of responsibility, our choice to move to the backdrop when someone is needed on the forefront.

I've always been curious about what inspired God when He created birds and animals. My personal experience led me to expect something different from what I had found. Have you ever noticed that among the same species of birds, often one is brown and the other one is full of color? The male is colorful, and the female camouflages herself into the backdrop. Now before we go any farther, I want to make clear that this is not true with the human species. We men are clearly the dull component of the two. Without question the female of the human species is the more colorful and attractive of the two.

With this said, let's go back and reflect on the reason for this phenomenon. The colors often found among the males serve at least two purposes. They attract females, and they intimidate any predators or rivals. The female carries the dull brown color for the purpose of camouflaging into the environment, which is necessary to avoid attracting danger to her nest and her young.

IT IS SO MUCH EASIER TO CHOOSE TO BE INVISIBLE. OH, THERE ARE OTHER WORDS FOR INVISIBLE— AVERAGE, MEDIOCRE, NORMAL, COMPLIANT, PREDICTABLE, SAFE—AND THE LIST COULD GO ON AND ON.

As human beings, we seem to have the choice about what feathers we wear. We can become dull for the purpose of avoiding any potential dangers and hide in the backdrop of life, or we can choose to take on colors, becoming more attractive to those around us and causing those who stand in our way to have second thoughts. It is so much easier to choose to be invisible. Oh, there are other words for *invisible—average, mediocre, normal, compliant, predictable, safe—*and the list could go on and on.

Sometimes we consciously choose to be invisible. At other times we seem to be trapped in invisibility. We want to be visible, but we can't figure out how to materialize. It's not that we're fighting for the limelight or want to be center stage; we just want our lives to mean something. Invisibility can be a safe place until we want to be seen. Eventually all of us long to be needed or cared for, loved or appreciated, and that requires visibility.

The most important decisions of our lives will require us to forsake invisibility and risk becoming visible. Whenever you choose to seize divine moments, you move from invisibility to visibility. Like Jonathan, you choose to go through the pass, to cross over toward the other side and let them see you. This story continued: "So both of them showed themselves to the Philistine outpost." They were at the point of no return.

THE MOST IMPORTANT DECISIONS OF OUR LIVES WILL REQUIRE US TO FORSAKE INVISIBILITY AND RISK BECOMING VISIBLE. WHENEVER YOU CHOOSE TO SEIZE DIVINE MOMENTS, YOU MOVE FROM INVISIBILITY TO VISIBILITY.

It is here that we enter the gauntlet that is found in our most profound divine moments. Not every moment is the same, nor does every moment have the same level of potential. Some moments carry within them the capacity to shape a lifetime. And this is the challenge that comes in those moments. The greater that moment's opportunity, the greater the risk required. This reality is fundamental to the Christian faith. There is no greater moment filled with eternal ramifications than the moment we turn from our sin and turn to Christ. In that moment, when we are invited to receive the infinite grace of God, we are required to give up everything we have. To have the life that Jesus Christ offers us, we must in that moment commit ourselves to die. If we are unwilling to die to ourselves, we are unable to receive the life that only God can give. The moment in which we have the most to gain is also the moment we have the most to surrender.

This truth is consistent to life itself: the greatest opportunities require the highest risk. If we want to live life to the fullest, we must be willing to trust God and risk everything. If heaven had an advertising section, it would take a full-page ad that read: "Wanted: Risk takers for God."

NO TURNING BACK

It was my first time to the Middle East. There were five of us traveling together through Egypt, Syria, Lebanon, and Turkey. We were divided into two vans as we were heading toward Sidon, one of the epicenters of the Muslim revolutionary group Hamas. As we made a quick stop to grab some food, one of the men from the other van ran to tell me that in a few hours I would be speaking to a group of Muslims. I was sure he was joking, some form of Lebanese humor. I quickly discovered he was absolutely serious. I was reassured that it would be just a small gathering of perhaps a dozen Christians and a handful of Muslims and that my topic was the history of Western Christianity.

That night when the event began, the small room was packed. Nearly eighty Muslims overwhelmed the handful of Christians who had organized the meeting. I was reminded before I spoke that these were first-time hearers of the gospel and that any declaration of Jesus being God would be considered nothing less than blasphemy. We were a short distance from the Palestinian refugee camp where people just months later would be shown celebrating the thousands of deaths at the World Trade Center. Los Angeles had given me many opportunities to engage people of Islamic backgrounds and beliefs, but this was totally different. In LA, I was in the majority with unlimited freedom to speak about my faith. Here I was in a clear minority, and the implications of sharing the gospel were dramatically different.

I must confess that I began with everything I could think of that they would agree with. I began to describe to them the Western Christianity that I had rejected. I understood that for many Muslims a nation is reflective of its religion. I understood that they saw no distinction between America and Christianity. In their minds Christianity produces MTV, Playboy, capitalism,

Hollywood—everything that comes from America. It made perfect sense to them when I described Western Christianity as materialistic and immoral. So far, so good. Everything I described up to that point reaffirmed their view of Christianity.

Then I began to explain that in the United States a revolution was taking place. It was a movement of sincere followers of Jesus Christ. They were members of what is called the church. This was different from Christianity as a world religion. It was a movement of faith, love, and hope. I explained the center point of this movement, what was called the gospel. As I came to a time of questions and answers, our host purposefully set me up. He asked me, "What is this true gospel that you keep speaking of?" And I proceeded to share the message that Jesus Christ had come into the world and offered them life.

There have been a thousand times in my life, perhaps tens or hundreds of thousands, when I have declared that Jesus Christ is Lord without a second thought. I have expressed that God Himself came into human history, took on flesh and blood, was crucified on our behalf, and was raised from the dead. I must tell you, this time was different. This same declaration had a greater weight to it than ever before. I thought deeply before I made my confession. I understood the implications and the potential consequence. Every person who stood up to ask me a question made me just a little bit nervous.

I think back with some amusement that one man who left his seat and walked to the front and began speaking to me face-to-face had a gun strapped to the back of his pants. My friends who were with me saw this scenario from a different perspective than I did. While I was looking into his eyes, my team was looking at his gun. I cannot express my delight that from what I thought was an audience expressing anger came a chorus of blessings toward my family and me. One man said, "As you were, I am," acknowledging that although he was Muslim, he did not know God and was searching for Him. Another man stood and said, "If there were Christians like you in Lebanon, this would be a much better nation." And he went on to say, "May you and your wife come to Lebanon and have many children." My wife, Kim, did not receive this blessing as from God.

Over the next hour, Muslim after Muslim came to me and to our team saying, "I would like to become a Christian." My friend from Lebanon who had orchestrated this meeting told me that I could not possibly understand the depth and miraculous nature of what was happening. Representatives from the Palestinian community gave me gifts and wrote me a letter thanking me for telling them about Jesus the Christ. I was overwhelmed by the warmth, graciousness, and openness of this Islamic community.

I did leave out one minor detail in this story. After the presentation, I sat down without inviting them to receive Jesus Christ as their Lord. I thought doing that might be pressing things a bit too far—or to put it more honestly, I might be pushing my luck. *After all*, I thought, *I did share the gospel with them, and that by itself is no small thing*. So I sat down, and the moderator began to close the meeting. Immediately I was haunted by the knowledge that I stopped just short of inviting them to give their lives to Jesus Christ and follow Him. It might have been because my heart was in my throat when I thought about doing that. And as I sat there, I knew I had missed a divine moment. God's window of opportunity formed right in front of me, and I refused to seize it.

Our host was closing the evening and thanking everyone for coming, and I just couldn't take it. I jumped out of my seat and apologetically went back to the front and asked the host if I could give one last word. I knew I needed to cross to the other side, to walk through the pass, to let them see me if I was going to fully seize this moment from God. And so against my better judgment, I invited those who were there to seize their divine moment and place their lives in the hands of Jesus Christ. It was this invitation that seemed to culminate the evening. I was letting them know that God was inviting them also to experience the fullness of His life.

Women and men who seize divine moments embrace the inherent dangers that come with them. Divine moments oftentimes require us to put our own well-being aside for the well-being of others, to relinquish our safe places for the sake of others. We can touch only those within our reach and can change only the world in which we live, but we can do that often. It requires us to move from the isolation of our invisibility to the dangers of visibility if we are going to make the invisible visible. That's the amazing thing about seizing divine moments. We choose to no longer be invisible, to take the risk of letting others see us, and so when we become visible, the invisible presence of God becomes visible.

IT REQUIRES US TO MOVE FROM THE ISOLATION OF OUR INVISIBILITY TO THE DANGERS OF VISIBILITY IF WE ARE GOING TO MAKE THE INVISIBLE VISIBLE. THAT'S THE AMAZING THING ABOUT SEIZING DIVINE MOMENTS.

Our action invokes God's activity. It is as if God is waiting for someone to trust Him enough to act on His Word. There is so much that God wants to do that can be seen only after we begin to do it. Sometimes we just don't realize how much latitude God gives us. In Philippians 4:8 Paul wrote, "Whatever is true, whatever is noble, whatever is right, whatever is pure, whatever is lovely, whatever is admirable—if anything is excellent or praiseworthy—think about such things." You see, whatever is within these parameters is fair game. Everything and anything! Think, dwell, enjoy, act on any of these that you want. They are all within the parameters of God's will for your life. Paul went on to say in the next verse, "Whatever you have learned or received or heard from me, or seen in me—put it into practice. And the God of peace will be with you." Again, we are commended to do whatever as long as it reflects the heart and character of God. Then a few verses later, he told us, "I know what it is to be in need, and I know what it is to have plenty. I have learned the secret of being content in any and every situation, whether well fed or hungry, whether living in plenty or in want. I can do everything through him who gives me strength" (Phil. 4:12–13).

DO YOU HEAR WHAT HE'S TELLING US? THINK ANY GOD THOUGHTS YOU WANT; DO ANY GOD DEEDS YOU DESIRE TO DO. DO IT BOLDLY, WHATEVER THE COST.

Do you hear what he's telling us? Think any God thoughts you want; do any God deeds you desire to do. Do it boldly, whatever the cost. Circumstances cannot rob you of the joy of life. And if you will give your life for God's risky business, you will find that you can do all these things through the power of Him who gives you strength.

FAIL-SAFE

Comedians love oxymorons. I'm sure you've heard of most of them, like "working vacation," "virtual reality," "instant classic," "passive aggressive," and "pretty ugly." A few I particularly like are "deliberately thoughtless," "friendly takeover," and of course, "idiot savant." Here's one that is rarely identified: "fail-safe." When something is considered fail-safe, sometimes that means it is guaranteed to work. At other times it is a deactivation term that promises that when improperly accessed, it is guaranteed to fail. So when something is fail-safe, it either promises not to disappoint you or promises to protect you. So much of our contemporary understanding of how God works emerges from a fail-safe paradigm. We have been taught that whenever God is in something, there is no chance for failure. At the same time we are reassured that when God is with us, we are guaranteed safety. In the process we create the most ironic oxymoron— "safe faith."

A fail-safe perspective blinds us to divine moments from several vantage points. We fail to see divine moments when all we see is danger and the risk of failure. We lose our confidence in the midst of divine moments when the journey becomes turbulent and God allows us to experience failure. And we are unable to celebrate divine moments, even after we've walked through them, if we look back and measure the success of the journey in human terms.

One of the advantages of the Scriptures is that it is predominantly a history book. We are able to look back and see what God has done. God's history in the story of humanity gives us a foundation for our present and future faith. Yet it is also a disadvantage that the text is predominantly a history book. It's like reading a book from the last chapter to the first. We know the ending of every story, even as we read the beginning. And beyond that we know the end of history, even as we live in the midst of it.

Whenever God is involved, the epilogue is not mysterious. God wins. Everyone on His side gets to share in that celebration. This is good news, but it can be terribly misleading. We think because the story concludes with a guaranteed victory, every chap-

WHENEVER GOD IS INVOLVED, THE EPILOGUE IS NOT MYSTERIOUS. GOD WINS.

ter is lined with nothing but victories. We expect our journey to look like a trip on a rocket ship beginning from the launching pad and reaching to the highest heavens. In fact, it is better described as a roller-coaster ride with nauseating ups and downs. We do well to remember that even in battles that are counted as victories, the winning side has many soldiers who died in the engagement. And so while the nation has a story of conquest, victory, and freedom, the individual might have a substory of conflict, suffering, and defeat. It is only because his life is interconnected to the broader story that his death gains both meaning and victory.

The divine moments are connected to eternal significance and may actually bring us greater pain in those moments. The journey that travels through divine moments is not an escape route from personal suffering. In fact, it strengthens our resolve to suffer in the now for the greater good that can be accomplished. It is a recognition that future moments are both born out of and connected to present choices. What we do in this moment has a direct relationship to the moments we know as our future. Concerning Jesus, the Scriptures say,

THE JOURNEY THAT TRAVELS THROUGH DIVINE MOMENTS IS NOT AN ESCAPE ROUTE FROM PERSONAL SUFFERING. IN FACT, IT STRENGTHENS OUR RESOLVE TO SUFFER IN THE NOW FOR THE GREATER GOOD THAT CAN BE ACCOMPLISHED.

"For the joy set before him [he] endured the cross" (Heb. 12:2). A misreading of this description of Jesus can make you think He was nothing more than a masochist. It is not difficult to see how even Christianity has misunderstood this description of Christ. The Scripture is not advocating suffering as a virtue. It wasn't the Cross that brought Jesus joy. Jesus wasn't saying pain was good or life is pain. It was the joy set before Him, the joy He knew was coming, the joy He could see through the Cross that gave Him the strength to seize that divine moment. Jesus embraced the suffering of the Cross through the strength that the joy brought Him.

We read in Nehemiah that the joy of the Lord is our strength (8:10). This is the wonder of a divine adventure. The strength of God comes in the form of joy, and the strength of that joy gives us the courage to face whatever cross we may have to bear. Divine moments are not fail-safe, and they are not risk-free.

It is always curious to me when someone says he has never failed. I know it seems impossible, but there are actually people who can say this. Certainly I'm not one of them. If anything, I'm in the failure business. If you happen to fall into that category of those with a perfect record, there are a few things you might want to consider. You cannot fail without risking. If you have never failed, it might just be possible that you have never risked.

Second, if you have never failed, you have never really lived. When you follow God, He takes you beyond your own capacities, forces you to go beyond your abilities. A part of the divine adventure is experiencing the miraculous hand of God as He intervenes in your life. Failure is often the context for miracles. We all want miracles, but we try to avoid **YOU CANNOT FAIL WITHOUT RISKING. IF YOU HAVE NEVER FAILED, IT MIGHT JUST BE POSSIBLE THAT YOU HAVE NEVER RISKED.**
needing them. But only sick people need healing, only people who are blind need to see, only people who are deaf need to hear, only people with leprosy need to be cleansed. No one else gets to experience these miracles firsthand. Wouldn't it be great to be Lazarus experiencing the power of God raising you from the dead? Of course, there is a downside. You have to die for this to happen.

Another aspect of failure is essential in the journey. Failure is a part of God's environment for shaping our character. I figured out a long time ago that God wasn't interested in our having a perfect season. He just doesn't seem to understand the downside of our experiencing failure. It becomes more than obvious the longer you walk with God that His teaching environment for us really is life. And allowing us to fail is not a punishment from God, but a part of God's process for shaping who we are. It is not a cliché to say that the road to greatness is paved by failure. Those men and women who would seize every divine moment must be willing to embrace failure as a part of life. Not as a part of existing. You can exist without ever failing, but you can't really live without facing it.

Those men and women who are characterized by the Jonathan Factor oftentimes even have a much higher failure rate than most others since they risk at a much higher rate. If it is difficult to fail without risk, it is even more difficult to succeed without failure.

BETWEEN ONCE UPON A TIME AND HAPPILY EVER AFTER

Divine moments live in between the sweet beginning and the savory ending. They exist between innocence and invincibility. In the midst of divine moments you are both most powerful and most vulnerable. This messy in-between is the context of your life. You do yourself a disservice when every story has a happy ending in this life. It's far more important that there be a meaningful middle. So often we're paralyzed in our fear to do the wrong thing, and it is important to always move forward with all the wisdom possible.

YOU DO YOURSELF A DISSERVICE WHEN EVERY STORY HAS A HAPPY ENDING IN THIS LIFE. IT'S FAR MORE IMPORTANT THAT THERE BE A MEANINGFUL MIDDLE.

But even Paul described his life as one where he saw through a glass dimly. He confessed that in this life he knew only in part. Too often we speak of God's will in shrouded terms. Our language betrays us. It is as if we long to know God's will, but God refuses to reveal it. He shrouds His will for our lives in mystery and then holds us accountable nonetheless. The kind of confidence that Jonathan displayed is built on the certainty that God moves through motivation far more than through information. The information given us in the Scripture is there for the purpose of formation. God never intended to give us a Book with every detail needed to live our lives. He gave us a Book with everything necessary to shape our lives. He was trying not to download heaven's database, but to make us user-compatible. When God has our hearts, we move naturally in His will. The fuel for a life of faith is more inspiration than information. It is not zeal without knowledge, but it is certainly not knowledge without zeal.

Risk that God respects is fueled by a passion for His purpose and a willingness to subjugate our lives to His mission. Prayer moves from *God, what is Your will for my life?* to *God, what is Your will, and how can I give my life to fulfill it?* In the midst of this process, there is a great deal of imperfection. It may be difficult to understand, but we can do the wrong thing for the right reasons. And we can do the right thing for the right reasons, and it comes out the wrong way (at least from our vantage point). All this is simply to say that Jonathan took a real risk that could have genuinely cost him his life, and in the same way our lives, when fully given to God, face similar possibilities.

In 1992 I moved to Los Angeles in part to head a project called LAZER. A team of us in LA began working on a project where a hundred churches would be started in the span of a summer. Kim and I sold our home and moved to Los Angeles from Dallas. There were no funding, no salary, and no people. Over the course of the next year, we drained every penny of our retirement and all of our personal resources to see this project succeed.

More than ten years before that, I sensed God leading me to Los Angeles. Kim and I were married with the understanding that one day we would move to LA. It was clear that Los Angeles was a critical primate city, and the potential for the spread of the gospel throughout the world from this place was almost unimaginable.

Everything seemed to line up in terms of God's heart. It was an important project. It aligned with God's character. It was strategic, and it failed. And by failure, I don't mean we fell short of our goals. It wasn't that we saw 96 churches out of 100 started, or even 70 or 80. Our disappointment wasn't from simply seeing 20 or 30 churches started. And it would be much easier even if I could say all we saw was a handful of churches started. The truth of the matter is that by the end of the period we had one small congregation emerging in Huntington Park, and that was only because I was down there trying to make it happen. The project, from a human perspective, was a dismal failure. And what made it more enjoyable was that the project had national attention. It seemed that people everywhere knew about LAZER. In the end, being the only one left, I had to fire myself and shut down the project.

If I were Cinderella, I could finish this story by telling you that the handsome prince showed up and made all my dreams come true. If I were Snow White, I could finish this story by telling you I finally woke up from my horrible nightmare. But in between "once upon a time" and "they lived happily ever after" is called now. And in the now there are all kinds of failures we have to live with. Failure can change us, shape us, teach us, and motivate us. Failure can be our friend. Failure is closely related to risk, which is closely related to success.

COUNTDOWN

When I came to Mosaic, we were a community church in east LA. With each year, our span of reach spread further throughout the entire city of Los Angeles. About seven years into the journey, it was clear we needed to venture northward. We had two services in east LA, one service in downtown LA, but an openness and receptivity from north LA was drawing attenders from this unexpected region of the city. People were driving down from Burbank, Glendale, Pasadena, and what we considered the remote valley.

But in all of our searching we couldn't find a place to meet. Finally we just did it. We began a countdown.

On a Sunday morning we announced that in seven weeks we were going to begin a new service north. When our community asked where, we said we had absolutely no idea. We just knew when and we knew why; we didn't know where or how. The call went out for the who—people who felt God was leading them to be a part of this venture. We were looking for fifty people who would become the core to start the new Sunday gathering. And then there were six weeks and no location, but we did find our fifty people. And then there were five weeks and no location. But we continued to train our new teams for the celebration. And then there were four weeks and no location, but the band began rehearsing and the greeting teams began to form. Then there were three weeks and no location, but we were highly motivated and prayer seems to work better when you're desperate. And then there were two weeks.

I have to admit, at two weeks I was getting a little nervous. Even the leadership team was feeling pretty anxious. *What if we don't find a property in two weeks? What are we going to do?* I remembered one of the churches we started years ago. We met outdoors in the downtown area of Fort Worth. We began to ask ourselves, "What would we do if we had no location? Would we cease to exist as a church? Are facilities necessary for our existence? Were we still confident that God was in this? Was this the response of the prompting of God's Spirit? Was this in line with God's mission? Would even our failure bring honor to God?" At every point the answer was yes. So we stood up and announced, "In two weeks we begin our service, even if we're homeless."

At the close of the morning service, a first-time guest named James offered to help in any way. He explained that he lived in north LA and would love to be of service. I had no idea who this man was, but I told him if he wanted to help, he could find us a place to meet. He didn't even blink an eye. His response was, "You need a place to meet? I know a company looking for a church to meet in its facility." He was a former employee of an editing company that operated out of that same facility on the second story of a brick building. They were two buildings of a strip club.

Within fourteen days of our launch date, we met with the owner of what we would soon call "the loft." They had been praying for a church to meet in the open area of their facility. We had been praying for an inexpensive place to meet in less than ten days. With one week to spare we were able to announce our new location. It seemed to be part of God's divine sense of humor that you would drive up a street and instead of turning right toward affluence, you would have to turn left and cross over to the wrong side of the tracks. When you see the sign "Nude, Nude, Nude," you turn right, go two buildings, and there you'll find Mosaic, Mosaic, Mosaic. With beanbags and futons furnishing the second-story loft, more than two hundred adults appeared in our first public service one week later. The countdown guaranteed the takeoff. Sometimes we wonder why we remain grounded. Could it be as simple as never beginning the countdown?

TO THE BEST OF MY UNDERSTANDING, FAITH IS TRUSTING GOD ENOUGH TO OBEY WHAT HE HAS SAID, AND HOPE IS HAVING THE CONFIDENCE THAT GOD WILL DO EVERYTHING HE HAS PROMISED. ONE PUSHES YOU; THE OTHER PULLS YOU.

There comes a time when you just gotta get up, get out from under the shade, pull your team together, and go to the point of no return. To the best of my understanding, faith is trusting God enough to obey what He has said, and hope is having the confidence that God will do everything He has promised. One pushes you; the other pulls you. They lead you into the wonder of experiencing divine moments. But without question, in between faith and hope, there is risk.

Long before September 11, I made it my personal mission to crusade against a long-standing Christian cliché. In *An Unstoppable Force,* I lament that it has become an accepted part of pop theology that the safest place to be is in the center of the will of God. I'm not saying that this statement is ill-intended, but it is misdirected and misinformed.

I have often thought about the motivation behind this statement. Maybe it was a concerned father or mother trying to comfort a small child. After all, when our children are afraid of the dark, don't we all try to comfort them with a sense of safety? Or maybe it was concerned parents watching their teenager run off to college. A sort of subtle warning, *Get out of God's will and you'll be in big trouble.* Whatever the motivation, the result has brought more damage than good. If the safest place to be is in the center of the will of God, then an appropriate measure of God's will is the test, *Is it safe?*

The inversion of this framework has clearly affected our Western faith. We have concluded that God promises safety. Those who are outside God's will, will experience danger. You cannot have risk and guarantee safety. Our pop theology has eliminated the place for risk and insulated us with a comfort-and-security theology. This view runs counter to what is found in the Scriptures. I want to reiterate the fact that the center of God's will is not a safe place, but the most dangerous place in the world. God fears nothing and no one. God moves with intentionality and power. To live outside God's will puts us in danger, but to live in His will makes us dangerous. (See *An Unstoppable Force,* pages 32–33.) When we begin to seize our divine moments, we do not begin to live risk-free, but instead become free to risk.

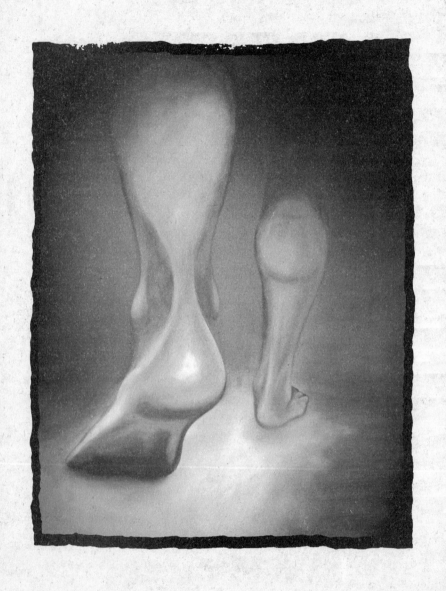

Ayden led the way as Kembr followed. With every step the path thickened in its darkness. Their eyes provided little help to them, but somehow they were more than able to find their way.

Everything carried its own heat and vibration. The darkness did not diminish the colors, which exploded from the degrees of warm and contrasting cold.

In the midst of silence they could feel the sounds all around them. Sounds so melodious they would sweep a traveler from his course to simply sit and listen. Yet behind them were cries of despair and even torment. It was becoming more difficult with every step to move forward. The darkness was almost suffocating.

Ayden interrupted Kembr's struggle with a stark reminder. "With one blow they have the strength to slay you. Fear will grip at you and strive to pull you back. They can do us no harm as long as we advance. They can only strike if we hesitate or step back."

Kembr confirmed his meaning: "Then to retreat is to ensure our death. Let us move forward then and live!"

— Entry 1223
The Perils of Ayden

6

ADVANCE

GO UNLESS YOU GET A NO

GROWING UP IN MIAMI MEANT THAT A PART OF physical education was having swim lessons. When you are virtually surrounded by water, knowing how to swim is an important part of survival. Each week as we spent that hour in the adjoining pool to the school we were faced with two major challenges. They were known as the low board and the high board. Pretty much everyone conquered the low board. It was just a short dive into the water. The high dive drew the line between the boys and the men.

For weeks I watched kids go off that board. All of them came up safely, and I could see that they were having a great time, but it just looked so high. And as I reflect on that experience, I realize a lot of girls were diving off that high board. The divide wasn't really between the boys and the men, but between the cowards and the courageous. I swam safely in the midst of the coward category.

One day I couldn't take it anymore. I had to experience what terrified me. I got in line, and the wait seemed to last forever to get to the ladder that would take me upward. As my hands touched the cold, wet steel and I began to climb, I could feel my heart pounding. I kept telling myself I could do it. I pushed myself beyond the ladder and stepped out on that white perilous board. I inched carefully to the very edge. I looked down and for the first time realized it was higher up than it appeared down below. Everyone was saying,

"Jump!" I was thinking, *Jump!* But my feet wouldn't move. I was paralyzed.

I considered my situation and decided there was only one thing to do. I turned around very carefully and walked my way back to the ladder. I was going to come back down, but there were two problems. The first one was the ton of kids hanging on the stairs waiting for me to jump. It was too crowded to go back. The second problem was the person behind me in line: my big brother. He looked at me and said, "You're not coming back this way." He made it clear there was only one way down and it wasn't going back, but going forward.

My anger that he wouldn't let me crawl back down became the fuel that gave me the courage to jump. I took a deep breath, swallowed my heart, and leaped to my death. I'm happy to say that I lived and actually enjoyed the experience.

I remember how desperately I wanted to go backward instead of forward and how I was willing to live with the humiliation of crawling my way back down the high-dive ladder. If I had done so, I would have never experienced the exhilaration of the dive and would have always lived with a boundary created by fear.

Life is full of high boards, the place we stand where we realize that the altitude is higher than we expected. The place where there is no neutral—we either go forward or go backward. Many times this becomes the dividing line, the line that separates those who see their divine opportunity and those who seize their divine opportunity. At this stage of the game you're close enough to taste it. You've made significant decisions to live out your divine adventure, but now you have to make a choice: Will you advance or retreat?

A DANGEROUS MOVE

That was the place where Jonathan stood. There was no turning back. The Philistines saw their enemy standing in the pass. Jonathan had already made a decision to go beyond the point of no return. He was clearly willing to die for the cause he was certain was right. Now we get a glimpse at the filter through which Jonathan understood the work of God.

Jonathan explained to his armor-bearer, "If they say to us, 'Wait there until we come to you,' we will stay where we are and not go up to them. But if they say, 'Come up to us,' we will climb up, because that will be our sign that the LORD has given them into our hands." Then they showed themselves to the Philistine outpost.

> "Look!" said the Philistines. "The Hebrews are crawling out of the holes they were hiding in." The men of the outpost shouted to Jonathan and his armor-bearer, "Climb up to us and we'll teach you a lesson." So Jonathan said to his armor-bearer "Climb up after me; the LORD has given them into the hand of Israel." (1 Sam. 14:11–12)

In terms of military strategy, genius would not describe Jonathan's idea. It goes without saying that you don't let the enemy see you, but he went beyond that irrational decision. He explained to his armor-bearer the strategy he had in mind: "If the Philistines decide to come down to us, we'll wait for them, but know that we're dead. If they call us up, if they challenge us to climb up the cliff and meet them in battle, that will be our sign from God that His victory is certain."

In any type of warfare, the side with the high ground has the advantage. If you can control the high ground, you can control the outcome. The logistics that Jonathan was describing would seem to make victory impossible. How could he expect to defeat the Philistines with one sword when he would have to use both hands and both feet to climb the cliff? His armor-bearer must have wondered whether Jonathan had either a death wish or information he had left undisclosed. Yet what we find in Jonathan's plan is not a shrewdly laid-out war plan. He was a servant who was convinced that God was more than ready to act.

Where Jonathan got this idea we cannot know for certain. But we do know it is consistent with how God had worked historically through His people, Israel. From the time of Abraham, they were a people commissioned to fulfill a mission. While their calling was specific, the application of that calling was always dynamic. Israel was called to worship the Lord only, and through the Israelites, He would bless the nations. Moses was used by God to lead Israel from Egypt to the banks of the promised land. Their journey stretched to forty years as a result of the wrong choices they made while they wandered in the wilderness. God's calling and promise to them were clear, yet their response shaped how the journey played out.

YET WHAT WE FIND IN JONATHAN'S PLAN IS NOT A SHREWDLY LAID-OUT WAR PLAN. HE WAS A SERVANT WHO WAS CONVINCED THAT GOD WAS MORE THAN READY TO ACT.

In the time of Joshua, the Lord again challenged His people to act on the promises He had made to them. He commanded Joshua to go and take possession of the land that the Lord would give them. Joshua was one of the twelve men selected to spy out the land and bring back a report. While ten of them reported that the land was filled with giants and discouraged invasion, Joshua and Caleb saw that the land was everything that God had promised. The ten were willing to relinquish the fulfillment of God's promise when they measured the weight of the challenge. Joshua and Caleb concluded that there could not possibly be enough giants to stop God from fulfilling His promise to them. If there were giants in the land, then a part of the mandate was to go to war. If the opponents were taller, stronger, more powerful, and more numerous than they were, that was God's problem. They had a calling to go and a promise to receive. The land was theirs if

GOD WOULD GIVE THEM VICTORY IN THE BATTLE, BUT HE WOULD NOT FIGHT THEIR BATTLE FOR THEM.

they would only take it. God would give them victory in the battle, but He would not fight their battle for them.

WHAT'S YOUR SIGN?

Jonathan was working from a conviction that he was already called to move forward. The army of God had already been charged with this mission. Victory over the Philistines was a promise simply waiting to be received. Jonathan was so confident his actions were in line with God's purpose that all he needed was a sign that said, "Advance." And he expected it to come from the strangest of all places—from the mouths of God's enemies. If the Philistines were arrogant enough to challenge them, that would be the sign that the Lord had given them into their hands. The only words he did not want to hear were, "Stay where you are." The call forward was the sign of victory. It was a call into danger. It was an invitation to engage in heated battle. He would be considered a fool by the measure of many, but from Jonathan's vantage point things were getting more interesting. He must have been thinking, *It just doesn't get any better than this!*

And so the Philistines saw them and began taunting Jonathan. They shouted out, "The Hebrews are crawling out of the holes they were hiding in." They mocked Jonathan and said to him and his attendant, "Come up to us and we'll teach you a lesson."

Any reasonable person would tremble in fear and run for his

life, yet Jonathan turned to his armor-bearer and said, "Climb up after me. The Lord has given them to us." You can almost hear the exhilaration in his voice: "This is the sign we were looking for." They were looking for a word to move forward.

We need to realize this is counterintuitive, but not "counter-faith." Somehow Jonathan understood that when you're moving with God, you must move with an advance mentality. You move forward unless God tells you to stop. You advance unless God tells you to wait. There are certain things that you do not need permission to do. You've already been commissioned to do them. There are certain things that you do not need a calling to do. You've already been commanded to do them.

Much of our religious language has been focused on the *don'ts* rather than the *dos*. In the same way we act as if the primary word from God is *stop* when it actually is *go*. Too many divine opportunities are lost because we keep waiting for a word when the word has already been given. For Jonathan *wait* was the kiss of death, and *come* was the sign from God. *Wait* made much more sense and took much less effort. *Come* implied increased effort and danger. Which leads to an important question, *What kind of sign are you looking for?*

Jonathan was moving forward in alignment with the purpose of God, and the challenge to advance was the affirmation of God's hand of power and blessing. He wasn't sitting around waiting for a sign. He moved forward in everything he knew to do. Confirmation came in the midst of action. He didn't point to the need for a sign as justification for fearful passivity or a subtle rebellion.

We have made a hero of Gideon and a model of his fleece before God. And while Gideon did many admirable things, we chose the wrong one to emulate. Gideon was confronted by the angel of the Lord with the greeting, "The LORD is with you, mighty warrior." His response was a question that many of us ask

God at different times in our lives, "If the LORD is with us, why has all this happened to us?" (Judg. 6:12–13).

The Lord responded with the word that is consistent throughout the Scriptures: "Go in the strength you have and save Israel out of Midian's hand. Am I not sending you?" (Judg. 6:14).

This is the intersection that we must cross: God begins with *go*, and we often begin with *wait*. It was because of Gideon's lack of trust in God, his lack of faith, that he placed a fleece before God. He placed a wool fleece on a threshing floor and said to God, "If You're going to save Israel by my hand, then bring dew only on the fleece and keep the ground dry." And so God did it. Gideon squeezed the fleece and filled a bowl with water.

> **THIS IS THE INTERSECTION THAT WE MUST CROSS: GOD BEGINS WITH *GO*, AND WE OFTEN BEGIN WITH *WAIT*.**

And then Gideon went, right? Wrong. He did it again. He tested God one more time. That time he wanted the fleece to be dry, and the ground covered with dew. And so the next night God did as Gideon asked.

It is amazing that God is so patient with us, that He doesn't give up on us with all the disbelief He has to face. Yes, God answered Gideon's fleece, but this is not supposed to be the model. When God says go, we should move without reservation. It is also important to note that God said to Gideon, "Go in the strength you have." That was why Gideon was afraid to go. He was well aware of how much strength he had and how much strength he didn't have. When we face God-sized challenges with man-sized capacity, we will want to fleece the entire herd and postpone the engagement. Yet this is a part of the adventure. God invites us to go in our own strength, trusting in Him and in our obedience receiving His strength.

In the end Gideon stepped up to the challenge. This should not lead us to believe that missed opportunities come without consequences. When the Israelites were called to step up to the challenge, they missed their moment, and it cost them forty years of their lives. Forty years when they could have been enjoying the land of promise they spent wandering a desert.

Is it possible that you have been fleecing your divine moments rather than seizing them? That you've said to God, "I'm not doing anything, risking anything, or going anywhere until You give me a sign"? Have you chosen to live in safety, comfort, and convenience, justifying this lifestyle because God hasn't called you to a different life? Is your justification for living a low-risk life the absence of a sign to live differently?

JUST SAY YES

Jonathan's sign was the taunting of a Philistine warrior. The only sign he needed was that God's will needed to be done, and he was in a position to try to do it. But what would happen if we changed our way of thinking? If we heard the first word of Jesus in His Great Commission, *Go*, as all the permission we needed to do the will of God? How would your life be different if you worked from a giant *YES* rather than a giant *NO*? While there are moments when God steps in and calls us to a specific task or assignment, even without that kind of special directive, we are not left without a

EVERY FOLLOWER OF CHRIST HAS THE PRIME DIRECTIVE OF REPRESENTING HIM ON THIS EARTH.

mission or calling. Every follower of Christ has the prime directive of representing Him on this earth. We are all called to be His witnesses. We are all commissioned to make disciples. We are all given the assignment of serving as His ambassadors of reconciliation. We are all commanded to love not only God, but also our neighbors as ourselves. We are all mandated to follow His example by serving others even as Christ has served us.

Several years ago one of our staff members was in a meeting relating to mission mobilization. A room full of women were processing what God's specific mission was for their lives. One of them listed a series of opportunities that she and her husband had considered. She described five or six different international opportunities and then explained that with each one God said no. Struck more by her framework of thinking than all the opportunities that were rejected, the staff member simply asked her one question: "Is there anything that God has said yes to you about?" And her startled response was, "I guess not." It can be incredibly frustrating when all you seem to be getting from God are the rejection slips. I look back now and realize it wasn't God who kept saying no.

What is it about our conversations with God that we seem to hear the no more readily than the yes? Many times when we claim we are waiting on God, He is waiting on us. It is true that Jesus instructed His disciples to wait in the Upper Room until they received the Holy Spirit. But then He instructed them that once they received the promise of God's Spirit, they were to move out and change the world. We, too, have received the Spirit of God and are expected to move out with confidence that God is with us.

MANY TIMES WHEN WE CLAIM WE ARE WAITING ON GOD, HE IS WAITING ON US.

Have you ever been stuck behind someone in traffic? Maybe on that day you were in a particular hurry, running late to an important engagement. There is just one car in front of you at the light. You're watching the light with an intense focus, waiting for it to change from red to green. It seems to take forever, but it finally comes to pass. You take your foot off the brake, you're just about to hit the gas, but you realize the person in front of you is entirely unaware that she has permission to go. Instead of looking forward, she is fixed on her own image in the rearview mirror. Remember what you were thinking? *Move, lady. It doesn't get any greener than this.* I wonder if that's what God is thinking?

The book of Acts certainly does not describe an apathetic people or even an apprehensive people. It describes a people on the move with God. They clearly moved from an advance mentality. They lived their lives fueled by the divine *yes*, and it was this God-inspired permission that made them an unstoppable force. This goes beyond proactivity and initiative. It is a sense of manifest destiny, a confidence that nothing can stop you from accomplishing God's purpose for your life. No challenge or enemy is powerful enough to stand in the way.

You are called not to be a survivor, but to be a conqueror. With passion and anticipation, you move with determination into the eye of the hurricane. This Jonathan Factor drives you to face the greatest challenges head-on rather than run from those challenges with your tail between your legs. I don't know what it means for others, but for a follower of Jesus Christ, what it means to live on the edge is to stand at the epicenter of where the kingdom of God confronts the kingdom of darkness. When evil raises its ugly head, taunting God and tormenting the weak, the adventurer rises up and moves toward the challenge. Like a guided missile, the adventurous spirit moves toward its greatest challenge.

I DON'T KNOW WHAT IT MEANS FOR OTHERS, BUT FOR A FOLLOWER OF JESUS CHRIST, WHAT IT MEANS TO LIVE ON THE EDGE IS TO STAND AT THE EPICENTER OF WHERE THE KINGDOM OF GOD CONFRONTS THE KINGDOM OF DARKNESS.

MESSING THINGS UP

What we also find in the book of Acts and in the writings of Paul is the messiness of real life. They didn't get everything right. The early Christian communities were far from perfect. No one, not even the apostles, had a perfect understanding. Many of us want a map, but what we get is a compass. We are not given a detailed outline of how we should live each day. We are given a due north, a direction we should move toward. On this journey one thing becomes certain: when you move forward on what you know, things become clearer. When you refuse to act on what you know, all that you do not know paralyzes you.

If you are a perfectionist, the adventurous journey will require additional retooling. Though we worship a perfect God, the journey is full of what you might consider unacceptable imperfections. The life of the adventurer is less like organizing an office and more like windsurfing. It is full of unknowable and unexpected variables. There is never a point where you can say the job is done until you reach the final destination.

Both in the Old Testament and in the New, the Spirit of God is described by the same word, which also translates *wind*. When we become a people of the Spirit, we join the wind of God as He moves through human history. You are going to make mistakes in

WHEN WE BECOME A PEOPLE OF THE SPIRIT, WE JOIN THE WIND OF GOD AS HE MOVES THROUGH HUMAN HISTORY.

this life, so make sure you make good mistakes. It is in that very weakness that God proves Himself strong. Even when we are committed to doing the good, we should not fool ourselves to think that we are doing the perfect. Yet in God's marvelous grace He strongly supports the work of those whose hearts are wholly His. In Paradise God gave man one *no* in the midst of an endless *yes.* Just one bad option and absolute freedom to choose from all the good as he preferred.

This is consistent with God's pattern for us, but now the stakes are higher. It's not just about choosing one of many good options; it's also about engaging the forces of evil that would consume all of humanity. The one bad tree has turned into a jungle. God is looking for adventurers who will fight their way through to rescue those who are lost in its darkness.

Those who seize their divine opportunities move with the God-given *yes* unless God says *no.* They work from the *go* and wait for the *stop.* They understand that the mission gives them permission. They know that the crisis encompasses their calling. They know that the danger is their invitation to step up to the challenge.

WHICH WAY ARE YOU LEANING?

In 1887 Elisha A. Hoffman wrote a song that has become part of classic American church life. Its name is "Leaning on the Everlasting Arms." The chorus goes like this:

Leaning, leaning, safe and secure from all alarms.
Leaning, leaning, leaning on the everlasting arms.

While I am certain that these words have brought comfort to countless millions over the years, it is at the same time an example of the direction we've been leaning for too long. The imagery that this great hymn gives us is one of leaning backward. It tells us if we lean on the everlasting arms of God, we will be safe and secure from all alarms. The implications are obvious. If you lean back into God's protective arms, He will not let anything hurt you.

I absolutely want to affirm that we should lean on the arms of God, yet I want to challenge both the direction of that leaning and its outcome. When you lean on the arms of God, you may find yourself in the most alarming situations, not safe from alarm. And even more important, when you begin leaning on God, you begin leaning forward rather than backward.

Several years ago I was introduced to a sociological phenomenon described as the adopter categorizations, which describe how quickly we respond to change. The bell-shaped graph basically tells us that 50 percent of the population lean forward and 50 percent of the population lean backward. In its more specific breakdown, it tells us that about 2 percent are called innovators, about 13 percent are early adopters, 34 percent are described as early majority, and 34 percent are late majority. About 13 percent are late adopters, and 2 percent are described as laggards.

In other words, about 15 percent of us are on the balls of our feet ready to move forward and about 15 percent of us are on the backs of our heels digging them in. In my years as both a student and a professor, I have been struck by how much of our hymnology and theology has been informed by the back end of this continuum.

Our language describing God has been more informed by the biblical images of God as our Rock, our Fortress, and our Stronghold. I'm sure that all of us have found comfort and strength from the attributes described in these expressions of our God. Yet we have not been as faithful in capturing other aspects of who God is as described through rushing wind and fire.

FALL FORWARD

A few winters ago a friend of mine named Bob was visiting us in Los Angeles. He invited me to go snow skiing with him, and it was something I had always wanted to do. I had been waterskiing for years, but I had never tried to ski on frozen water. This would be a first.

We went over to the Big Bear area, and I signed up for one of those beginners' classes, one of those comprehensive training schools that lasts fifteen to thirty minutes. They cover the full gambit of the skiing experience from how to put on your skis and stand up without falling to how to board the lift and dismount without falling, and of course, how to get up after you have fallen from both experiences.

After the brief instruction, Bob came over and led me to one of the lifts so I could have my first downhill experience. Some of the instructor's words remained fuzzy to me, but one set of instructions was very clear: "You're a beginner. The green circle is where you stay. Wait until later in the day to try the blue square. And do not, I repeat, do not go to the black diamonds."

As we mounted the lift and it began pulling us up the hill, I assumed there were different places that I could dismount. I could get off at the green section or wait until the blue section or ride it to the top and come down the black. I quickly learned this is not how the lifts are organized. Each lift has one destination. I soon learned from Bob this was the black diamond lift. My first experience down a slope was a black diamond. Bob kept swearing to me he put me on there by accident. I have to believe him since he is a pastor.

I had one simple strategy on the way down. Aim toward what looked like the softest snowdrift, and head that way. When I made it to the bottom, I felt that I had accomplished an unbelievable feat and immediately headed toward the blue section. After all, I survived the black diamond. I only crashed ten or twelve times. The blue would be nothing.

When I got off the lift on the blue, I pointed my skis downward and realized I had no idea how to move side to side. Careening down the hill in a straight line, taking the shortest route between two points, I went down that hill wide open with no way to stop except to crash. The momentum took me right up to the patio area of the ski lodge where I finally came to a slow stop. An instructor came over to me and told me he had never seen anyone take that hill wide open. He thought it was amazing. I explained to him that I couldn't stop and I was afraid to fall.

On my way down, I just kept thinking, *Bend your knees and lean forward.* At that point no other instructions really mattered except, *Don't lean back; lean forward.* This is good advice for all of us who are novices of the divine adventure: lean in the direction that you're supposed to go. Recognize that when you put

GOD'S INSTRUCTIONS ARE TO GO, LIVE LIFE, TAKE RISKS, MOVE FORWARD, ADVANCE.

on your kingdom skis, God sends you in a specific direction. And yes, you must get off the lift. God's instructions are to go, live life, take risks, move forward, advance.

A DIVINE INVITATION

In 1991 Kim and I were having to make another significant decision in our life together. Was it time for us to move from Dallas to Los Angeles and begin a new adventure with God? In many ways the decision was much more difficult at that stage than it ever had been before. There was so much to give up, so much to lose.

When we were first married, it was pretty much just us. We didn't own a whole lot, and we didn't have any children to consider. Advancing was just so much simpler then. Now we had a three-year-old boy, and Kim was pregnant with our second child. My work as a denominational consultant had come to a close, and the result of our work had brought us significant financial security. In just a few years we had gone from renting an apartment and sleeping on the floor to owning a brand-new home and being able to buy a new car with cash. But it seemed that God was inviting us to give it all up and start afresh.

As we were working our way through this decision, Kim had a unique encounter with God through the Scriptures. She came to me later with tears in her eyes and read to me Luke 14:15–24:

When one of those at the table with him heard this, he said to Jesus, "Blessed is the man who will eat at the feast in the kingdom of God."

Jesus replied: "A certain man was preparing a great banquet and invited many guests. At the time of the banquet he sent his servant to tell those who had been invited, 'Come, for everything is now ready.'

"But they all alike began to make excuses. The first said, 'I have just bought a field, and I must go and see it. Please excuse me.'

"Another said, 'I have just bought five yoke of oxen, and I'm on my way to try them out. Please excuse me.'

"Still another said, 'I just got married, so I can't come.'

"The servant came back and reported this to his master. Then the owner of the house became angry and ordered his servant, 'Go out quickly into the streets and alleys of the town and bring in the poor, the crippled, the blind and the lame.'

"'Sir,' the servant said, 'what you ordered has been done, but there is still room.'

"Then the master told his servant, 'Go out to the roads and country lanes and make them come in, so that my house will be full. I tell you, not one of those men who were invited will get a taste of my banquet.'"

It was the parable of the great banquet. This parable became more to us in that moment as Kim began to share. Not only has God invited all of us to feast with Him in the kingdom of God, but God was inviting us specifically to join Him at His banquet. With tears in her eyes Kim explained, "God is inviting us to join Him in a celebration. He's throwing the party in Los Angeles. He has everything prepared, even though we cannot see it. If we don't go, there will be two empty seats there."

The parable is a stark reminder that there are so many lost opportunities, the lost opportunity of rejecting God's invitation to know Him through His Son, Jesus Christ, and yes, the endless opportunities lost when we ignore God's invitation for us to join Him in what He is doing, where He is doing it. In a very real way, God is throwing a party, and we are invited. Its participants are those who hear God's invitation and seize their divine moments.

IN A VERY REAL WAY, GOD IS THROWING A PARTY, AND WE ARE INVITED. ITS PARTICIPANTS ARE THOSE WHO HEAR GOD'S INVITATION AND SEIZE THEIR DIVINE MOMENTS.

Like those who miss the party, we are all full of excuses. One said, "I just bought a field. I must go see it. Please excuse me." Another said, "I have just bought five yoke of oxen. I am on my way to try them out. Please excuse me." Another said, "I just got married, so I can't come." Same old excuses. I have places to go, things to do, and people to see. I am just too busy to accept God's invitation to life. I do think it is funny that the first two said, "I choose not to come," but the one who just got married said, "I'm not allowed to come."

It is amazing how often the very ones who are supposed to encourage us to move forward are the ones who hold us back. I've personally known so many women whose hearts are filled with God's passion and yet find themselves unable to seize divine moments because of the passivity of their husbands.

Our lives should be filled with friends and family members who long to move forward and capture all the life that is to be experienced. This is one characteristic that makes Mosaic so special to me. We are a community of people on our toes rather than our heels. There is something exciting about an entire community leaning forward to advance the good on God's heart rather than leaning back, attempting to resist it.

GET PACKED AND READY

One of the most asked questions about Mosaic is, *How are we able to mobilize so many people to overseas missions?* It's really pretty easy to explain. If your church is full of members, you get an occasional missionary. If your church is full of missionaries, the rest is just about geography. Most churches don't send missionaries because they don't have any. We have for several years averaged nearly one adult a month moving as a career missionary into what is known as the ten-forty window where the most unreached people in the world live. These were not people suddenly called to missions; these were people who were already on missions, and then God chose a change of address.

One of the most exciting periods in our church's history was a thirteen-month span when more than 50 percent of our average attendance left the United States on some kind of mission or service project. During that year we received a call for help from a team of missionaries in the region consisting of China and Mongolia. They had their annual meeting coming up in just a few months where more than five hundred workers would come together.

The regional leader explained to me the comprehensive nature of their need for that ten-day period. The meeting was one year of church concentrated into just a few days. I was already scheduled to be the speaker, and he was asking if I could bring a team.

"Worship team?" I asked.

He said, "Yes."

"How about drama and creative arts?"

He said, "That would be great."

"Anything else you need?"

He said, "Well, preschool workers would be helpful."

"Anything else?"

"Well, a children's ministry is very much needed." He went on to tell me junior high and high school workers were also on the list. When he finished listing all the different needs for their annual retreat, the number jumped to approximately forty people.

It was so outrageous to think that our spiritual community of maybe six hundred adults could mobilize forty trained professionals to give up two weeks of their vacation, raise more than $40,000, and go to Asia to change diapers, that we went ahead and said, "Sure, we'll do it." I wish I could tell you that it was really difficult, that it took me months of diligent effort to pull the team together, but it took less than an hour to get all the buy-in I needed. It probably wasn't two weeks later that we had our complete team of forty-two. It was virtually effortless to pull together the nearly $40,000, although it did require real sacrifice on the part of many people. This would never have been possible if I had to begin with members and turn them into missionaries.

It would have been impossible to take people whose heels were dug in and move them to the balls of their feet with this kind of notice. You cannot advance the kingdom of God with people who are in retreat.

YOU CANNOT ADVANCE THE KINGDOM OF GOD WITH PEOPLE WHO ARE IN RETREAT.

Every one of us, like Jonathan, can live from an advance mentality. We can lean forward on God's everlasting arms.

DEFY YOUR FEARS

My brother, Alex, has had a phobia about flying as long as I can remember. As children we began flying as early as the age of five.

We would go back and forth from El Salvador to the United States. Alex, being older, would always get the window where we both preferred to sit. I soon learned there was no point in fighting over the window since just after takeoff, Alex would be running to the back of the plane to spend the bulk of his time in the bathroom. I'm not sure if his flying phobia is directly related to his childhood experience, but flying has never been one of his favorite means of transportation.

As we began working together in ministry, he explained that he did not appreciate my invitations to travel. In fact, he explained to me that they actually made him angry. It wasn't just that he didn't enjoy flying or that he feared flying; he hated flying. As he would put it, "I'm not afraid of flying; I'm afraid of crashing." And this was all before September 11.

Then something strange happened. When two planes crashed into the World Trade Center and two others crashed on the East Coast, we found a nation afraid to fly. Countless events throughout the country have had reduced numbers of participants and have even been canceled as a result of our newfound crisis. Yet for Alex, the exact opposite became true. He said he was standing near the campus of USC and saw a plane flying over. It was the first passenger plane he had seen since the attack of September 11. He said in that moment he knew that he was watching an act of defiance, that once being a passenger took very little forethought, but now it required a conscious decision to move forward rather than remain paralyzed.

Since then my brother has never been the same. He has been on planes multiple times. No phobia, no fear, just pure defiance—leaning forward, seizing the divine moments, advancing the kingdom of God. It was as if he heard the Philistines say, "Come up to us and we'll teach you a lesson." He heard it as a sign from God that the Lord had called him to advance.

Jonathan wasn't simply defying the odds; he was defying fear itself. Nothing would stop him from moving forward and doing what was right. What would our world look like if we were a society full of Jonathans?

TAKE THE CHALLENGE

I'll never forget the panic of Y2K. It seemed that all around us was an accelerating sense of doom. Certainly it was not one of American Christianity's best moments. Christian literature seemed only to capitalize on the hysteria. Very little was being written or said to try to bring perspective and positive direction. Our appetite for apocalyptic literature seemed only to fuel the frenzy. I wonder how many Christians have been left with thousands of dollars of tuna and nonperishables. Thoughtful Christians were making irrational decisions, such as leaving their homes and moving toward isolated shelters. Churches around the nation were looking for spiritual leadership to lead by example and to give biblical perspective.

NO PHOBIA, NO FEAR, JUST PURE DEFIANCE—LEANING FORWARD, SEIZING THE DIVINE MOMENTS, ADVANCING THE KINGDOM OF GOD.

As a family we made a decision. We would not submit to the hysteria of the moment. We would tell our community to lean forward. The world was not coming to an end. We needed to develop a strategy that would advance God's purposes into the twenty-first century.

In the midst of this crisis, God gave us a perfect opportunity to put our action where our mouths were. I was invited to speak in different parts of the country during the millennial transition, and so we flew to Philadelphia. I spoke at the birthplace of our nation and then flew to Houston and spoke to thousands of students who ushered in the new year together, and on January 1, I flew home with my wife and two children to Los Angeles. As a declaration of our confidence in God's future, we took a coast-to-coast-to-coast journey and then spoke that next morning on engaging the third millennium.

If you're going to seize divine moments, you must be willing to face your giants. Remember, the Philistines were the people of giants. That was the family of Goliath and his brothers. Jonathan stepped up to the moment even before David would take Goliath's head. I guess you could say you have to slay the giant if you're going to get a head.

After risk comes advance. After "no turning back" comes "you must go forward." The closer you get to a divine challenge, the bigger it will seem, and the smaller you will feel. If the signs you are looking for are guarantees of success, you may retreat when you should be advancing. It would be great if the signs from God that we should advance were always things like a perfect situation, all the resources necessary to succeed, or a guaranteed win. Yet if that were the case, there would be no adventure.

AFTER RISK COMES ADVANCE. AFTER "NO TURNING BACK" COMES "YOU MUST GO FORWARD." THE CLOSER YOU GET TO A DIVINE CHALLENGE, THE BIGGER IT WILL SEEM, AND THE SMALLER YOU WILL FEEL.

Besides, that isn't reality. More often than not the signs pointing us to advance will be ominous. They will cause us to assess who we are and who we believe God to be. They will make clear our priorities. Are we in it for what we can get or for what we can give? The signs will expose our hearts, reveal our fears, and unleash our faith. There is a word for the mind-set of those who seize divine moments—*advance*. The night may be coming, but they are chasing daylight. They not only refuse to run from the challenge, they run with full force toward it.

AFTERSHOCK

Creation groans for all to be set right.

The earth roars in violence — disrupting what is to make room for

what is to come.

Only after everything is shaken can it find its rightful place.

Its movement destroys, divides, and defines. Even the mountains

tremble.

Yet there is a kingdom that remains.

— Maven

The Perils of Ayden

Jonathan climbed up, using his hands and feet, with his armor-bearer right behind him. The Philistines fell before Jonathan, and his armor-bearer followed and killed behind him. In that first attack Jonathan and his armor-bearer killed some twenty men in an area of about half an acre.

Then panic struck the whole army—those in the camp and field, and those in the outposts and raiding parties—and the ground shook. It was a panic sent by God.

Saul's lookouts at Gibeah of Benjamin saw the army melting away in all directions. Then Saul said to the men who were with him, "Muster the forces and see who has left us." When they did, it was Jonathan and his armor-bearer who were not there.

Saul said to Ahijah, "Bring the ark of God." (At that time it was with the Israelites.) While Saul was talking to the priest, the tumult in the Philistine camp increased more and more. So Saul said to the priest, "Withdraw your hand."

Then Saul and all his men assembled and went to the battle. They found the Philistines in total confusion, striking each other with their swords. Those Hebrews who had previously been with the Philistines and had gone up with them to their camp went over to the Israelites who were with Saul and Jonathan. When all the Israelites who had hidden in the hill country of Ephraim heard that the Philistines were on the run, they joined the battle in hot pursuit. So the LORD rescued Israel that day, and the battle moved on beyond Beth Aven.

— 1 Samuel 14:13–23

"What weapons have you brought?" Kembr asked Ayden as she felt the conflict drawing near.

"There were no weapons to bring," Ayden explained.

"And, Maven, he would let us come defenseless?" Kembr asked in disbelief.

"We did not come to defend but to conquer," Ayden declared, as if he missed the point. "We are both warrior and weapon." Ayden went on, "There is but one hope against the shadows, and that is the light within us. If it is not enough, there is no blade sharp enough to cut the thick darkness."

Kembr's steps felt heavy as she walked. Is this how fear paralyzes you? she thought to herself. Yet with every step it seemed as if the ground would tremble. Or was it her?

"What is happening beneath me?" she shouted to Ayden as the earth below shook with increasing force.

"It is the density of the light!" Ayden yelled back with excitement. "It is the weight of the Presence!"

— Entry 1771
The Perils of Ayden

7

IMPACT

LEAVE A MARK

REMEMBER THE OLD CLICHÉ THAT IF GOD CLOSES A door, He opens a window? Have you found yourself wasting too much time sitting on the wrong side of the closed door, trying to figure out when God is going to build the window to facilitate your escape? Let me make a simple observation that could change everything for you: there are a lot more walls than there are doors and windows.

This is not to say we don't come to this dilemma without cause. Every once in a while we get an opportunity, a moment that is so sweet it is virtually impossible to miss. There's nothing subtle about it. It just comes at us like a fastball racing for the sweet spot on our bat, a moment so full of possibility that even we couldn't mess it up.

It's like me asking Kim to marry me. I did it all wrong, but she still said yes. I remember the night we were sitting in her car, and I was about to give her an engagement ring. I spent about an hour setting up the moment. No, not painting a picture of our unending love, but developing a theological discourse against materialism. This is what happens when a seminary education and natural male stupidity come together in one moment. I made her feel so bad that when I presented her with the ring, she refused to take it. I was shocked that she would respond that way to my generosity and my obvious symbol of love. Yet even with numerous blunders of this kind, she was still willing to marry me. Love is funny that way. It really does overlook a multitude of sins—and stupidity. Asking Kim to marry me was not only a divine moment, but one of life's defining moments. It was a moment that had lifelong implications.

Those open doors and windows of opportunities are wrapped around what appears to be perfect timing. It's what is often described as being at the right place at the right time. It's walking in with your résumé five minutes after the employer had someone with your qualifications quit. It's finally going to share the message of Jesus Christ with a friend who just prayed to God, *If You're out there, give me a sign.* It's working backstage during auditions, and suddenly they decide you have the look they've been searching for.

But unfortunately it isn't always like this. Most divine moments need to be seized, not simply walked through. There are many times in our lives when we thought one opportunity was God's door and then found that it was shut at the very last moment. In the midst of our discouragement we find God creating a new opportunity we never imagined—that would be the window. Yet many times what we find are closed doors, locked windows, long corridors, endless hallways—in other words, lots of walls. It's pretty easy to see the doors of opportunity, and it is always exhilarating when windows of opportunity open before us. What can be missed are the endless divine opportunities hidden behind the walls that can be discovered only if we go through the walls.

Some of life's greatest opportunities are not behind doors or windows, but behind walls. They require genuine effort. Beyond risk they require real sweat. Our religious integration of Christianity with capitalism and consumerism has resulted in a view of life that says if God is in it, it comes easily. Then when the inevitable difficulties come, when we hit the wall, we either assume God is not in it or conclude we've made a wrong choice in our pursuit.

I've become convinced over the years that the most important moments to seize, the most significant God opportunities, are the ones that do not come easily. Even when they begin easy enough, oftentimes they become far more complex and difficult in the later phases. It shouldn't surprise us that giving ourselves to great things comes with a cost. After all, if divine moments were that easy to seize, everyone would be living the abundant life of which Jesus spoke.

BEHIND ENEMY LINES

Samuel told us that after Jonathan received his sign from God, he climbed up using his hands and feet with his armor-bearer right behind him. He went on to tell us that the Philistines fell before Jonathan. In the first attack Jonathan and his armor-bearer are recorded to have killed twenty men in the area of about a half acre. That was real war. Not a metaphor, but a battle with real blood, real wounds, real pain, real suffering, and real death.

In this particular situation it was war between the Israelites and the Philistines. God was establishing for Himself a people through whom He would invite the nations to Himself. The Philistines expressed both an idolatry and an immorality that God would not allow Israel to assimilate or embrace. In this first encounter alone, Jonathan's "army" was outnumbered twenty swords to one. Whatever faith Jonathan might have had at that moment moved from theory to practice. He was engaged in a battle, and one properly directed weapon would end his life. Jonathan understood a basic reality: you cannot be a people of conquest if you're unwilling to enter the battle.

You can talk all day about what God has promised to do through

His people, but you will never live in those promises until you act on them. And if you act on the promises of God, if you choose to seize divine moments, it will eventually happen. It is unavoidable. There will come a moment of impact when your insistence will meet the world's resistance.

This might well be the moment you ask yourself, *What am I doing here? What was I thinking? Is there any way out of this mess I've created?* The account doesn't tell us what Jonathan was thinking in that moment. It doesn't list

YOU CAN TALK ALL DAY ABOUT WHAT GOD HAS PROMISED TO DO THROUGH HIS PEOPLE, BUT YOU WILL NEVER LIVE IN THOSE PROMISES UNTIL YOU ACT ON THEM.

for us the countless reservations or endless second-guessings that were racing through his mind. He did briefly explain to his armor-bearer that things could go wrong. He explained, "If they say to us, 'Wait there until we come to you,' we will stay where we are and not go up to them." Jonathan was telling his young apprentice, "If the evidence indicates that things are not going to go well, that we are going to die in a failed effort, we will not run. We will await our destiny with courage." Jonathan did not have the advantage we have of knowing the end of the story. And if the exhilaration of the sign to advance is any indication, the moment before as he held his breath must have been filled with uncertain tension.

This is where it is safe to say there is something specific about the Jonathans in the world. While everyone else was sleeping, Jonathan was engaged in the battle. And while he was closest to death, he was in a very real way the only one who was truly alive. He refused to sleep through this divine opportunity. Because of this, he became both the lightning rod and the flagship of God's activity.

My son, Aaron, was about four years old when the nightmares began. They terrified him to such an extreme that he would run out of his room and beg to find safety in our bed. He kept insisting that there were giant elves jumping up and down on his bed. I know kids have vivid imaginations, but this seemed particularly unusual to me. I did what most of us do as dads. I tried to explain to him that there were no giant elves in the room, and if there were, why would they want to jump up and down on his bed and bother him? But nothing seemed to work. The nightmares recurred night after night.

Kim and I strained ourselves to understand what was going on. Then all of a sudden it occurred to us. It became so clear, we were surprised we didn't see it right away. Just a few days earlier the Reseda earthquake had hit us here in Los Angeles. Although our home in Alhambra was left entirely undamaged, the quake had shaken it like a rag doll. We never thought to talk about it very much, but apparently it had terrified our little boy. He had translated his experience and reinterpreted it through his dreams.

Once I realized what was going on, I quickly tried to explain it to him. I told him there were no elves. It was an earthquake. It shook the ground and scared everybody. It didn't help. The nightmares continued—until Saturday. I knew what I needed to do. I put Aaron in the car, and we joined a team from Mosaic that went into Northridge to work with the thousands who were displaced and traumatized at the epicenter. We served people food, gave them water, helped them with survival packages, talked and prayed with people. We did whatever we could to help alleviate their suffering. Aaron was right there serving those in need, and that night he slept like a baby. No more nightmares. In a very real sense we took him into the mouth of the dragon so that he could overcome his fears.

I am convinced that when we face our fears, we look straight into the eyes of opportunity, and the courage we often need to engage our greatest challenge can be found only in the midst of engaging that challenge. There is a point as we seize our divine moments that a battle begins. It is in this point of impact where we experience conflict, opposition, and resistance. But it is also at this point of impact where we have the greatest opportunity. It is on the battlefield that we reflect what's on God's heart, and we stand in that place where God longs to make Himself known.

WHAT ARE YOU DOING HERE?

Remember when Elijah was running away from Jezebel? It's hard to imagine a man who just prayed fire down from heaven hiding in fear from a secondhand threat. In one moment Elijah was standing on Mount Carmel. He stood face-to-face against 450 prophets of a god named Baal and 400 prophets of a god named Asherah. All 850 were the demonic warriors of the evil queen Jezebel. Though he stood alone, Elijah fearlessly opposed them and called the people of Israel to reject Jezebel's reign and follow the Lord God only. He challenged her prophets to a duel of fire. They would build two altars. The prophets of Baal and Asherah would pray to their gods. They would call upon their gods to send fire from heaven and consume the altar.

Then Elijah would do the same. He would call on the name of the living God and ask Him to consume the altar. He called the people to witness this conflict of heaven and hell and challenged them to acknowledge that whichever god answered with fire—He is God. The people agreed.

And so the challenge began, and Jezebel's prophets went first. They called on their god. They shouted, but there was no response. They danced around the altar they had made in hopes of inspiring their god to action. There was nothing. Elijah taunted them. He told them to shout louder. He said to them, "Surely he is a god! Perhaps he is deep in thought, or busy, or traveling.

Maybe he is sleeping and must be awakened" (1 Kings 18:27). It is implied in the text that Elijah was alluding to a god with spiritual diarrhea stuck in the toilet unfortunately indisposed. Hearing this spurred them on to more desperate petition.

They shouted louder and even slashed themselves with swords and spears, as was their custom, until their blood flowed freely. The day passed on, but all their desperate attempts to move their god remained unanswered. In the end, no one answered.

Then Elijah called the people together. He repaired the altar of the Lord. He pulled together twelve stones, which represented the twelve tribes of Israel. He dug a trench around the altar. He arranged the wood, cut the bull into pieces, and laid them on the altar. Then he instructed the people to fill four large jars of water. He told them to pour it over the offering and the wood. And then he instructed them to do it again. And then a third time.

After water was running down the altar, everything drenched and the trenches filled to the brim, Elijah prayed to the Lord God. He simply acknowledged who God is, identified himself as a servant of the Lord, confessed that he was only acting out of obedience to what God commanded, and then asked God to act. He prayed, "Answer me, O LORD, answer me, so these people will know that you, O LORD, are God, and that you are turning their hearts back again" (1 Kings 18:37). With undaunted confidence, he called on God to send fire, and immediately God did. First Kings 18:38 tells us, "Then the fire of the LORD fell and burned up the sacrifice, the wood, the stones and the soil, and also licked up the water in the trench."

Then the unexpected happened. With Elijah at the pinnacle of his ministry, we find this man of unbelievable faith lying at the bottom of a spiritual gutter. Jezebel heard what happened to her prophets and, through a messenger, threatened to kill him. Unexplainably Elijah was afraid and ran for his life. After wandering for a brief time in a desert and struggling with suicidal thoughts, Elijah found himself in a cave on Mount Horeb. While he was hidden in the cave, God came and asked him a very important question, "What are you doing here, Elijah?" (1 Kings 19:9). Elijah had seized many divine moments, but he had hit the wall. Overwhelmed and exhausted, he felt he just couldn't go on. God's solution was simple. He commanded Elijah to "go out and stand on the mountain in the presence of the LORD, for the LORD is about to pass by" (1 Kings 19:11).

As God passed by, there was a great and powerful wind followed by an earthquake, which was followed by fire, and Elijah explained He was not in any of those. God, we find, was only in a still, small voice asking Elijah, "What are you doing here?"

Whenever we run from the challenges that God sets before us, He asks us the same question, "What are you doing here?" Whenever we settle for a life of mediocrity, God asks us the same question, "What are you doing here?" Whenever we decide that the average is good enough, God asks us, "What are you doing here?" Whenever we settle for simply existing, God asks us, "What are you doing here?"

THE SOLUTION IS TO STOP RUNNING AND HIDING FROM GOD AND TO LISTEN ONCE AGAIN TO HIS VOICE. WHEREVER YOU ARE, GOD WILL FIND YOU. THIS IS NOT A THREAT; THIS IS A PROMISE.

The solution is to stop running and hiding from God and to listen once again to His voice. Wherever you are, God will find you. This is not a threat; this is a promise. When He comes to you and passes by, don't just stand there; go with Him. Remember, God is doing something in human history. When we run from His purpose, we run from His presence. Do not be surprised if in your fear and weakness, He challenges you to get up and be strong. For the same God who has come to heal you will also lead you back into the battle. He will call you to engage the enemy of His purpose and fulfill your God-given destiny. He will send you back to face your fears.

There are times when we are called to go forward, and the worst thing we can do is to retreat from the challenge before us to the safety behind us. There are other times when the most courageous thing we can do is to go back. When we have run away from a God-given challenge, we must go back to go forward. The next thing the Lord said to Elijah was, "Go back the way you came" (1 Kings 19:15). The only way Elijah could move forward was to go back, to finish what he left incomplete, to step into the dark places and bring the light of God's presence. What we sometimes miss is that God desires to reveal Himself through the choices we make. If we run from the battle, it is difficult for God to win the battle through us. It is imperative that we choose to go where God is longing to work. The right instrument in the wrong place is a terrible tragedy.

We read in 2 Chronicles 16:9: "For the eyes of the LORD range throughout the earth to strengthen those whose hearts are fully committed to him." That's exactly who Jonathan was: the heart that was wholly God's, standing just in the place where God would have him. And in that moment, in the midst of the battle, when all odds were against him, the eyes of the Lord saw him, and God's strong support quickly followed. Samuel wrote, "Then panic struck the whole army—those in the camp and field, and those in the outposts and raiding parties—and the ground shook. It was a panic sent by God!"

Jonathan moved with God, and God moved with Jonathan. It may sound strange, but God joined Jonathan's effort. It wasn't that Jonathan changed God's mind, but in fact that Jonathan expressed God's heart. He did what was on God's mind, and his action created an opportunity for God to act on his behalf. The tables quickly turned from Jonathan and his armor-bearer against the armies of the Philistines to Jonathan, his apprentice, and the living God against the enemies of God's purpose.

Samuel described a total confusion among the Philistines as they were striking each other with their own swords. Because Jonathan became a warrior for God, God became a warrior for Jonathan. Samuel wanted to make sure there was no ambiguity about who sent the earthquake. It was not an incidental, natural disaster that came at a timely moment. The earth shook, and it was a panic sent by God. Jonathan was willing to live on the edge, and God had made him the epicenter. His life marked where God was moving. God wanted to make sure that everyone understood that this man's life reflected what God was doing in history.

WILLING TO STAND ALONE

The technical definition of *impact* is "a forcible contact between two or more things." This is an accurate description of how men and women are used by God to shape the course of human history. Whenever God is doing a new thing, He does it through people. And those He chooses to lead the way are

IT IS A PRIVILEGE TO BE CALLED TO GO FIRST EVEN WHEN IT MEANS YOU ARE THE FIRST TO SUFFER AND THE ONLY ONE AT RISK.

often considered fortunate only in retrospect. The reality in the moment is often quite different. It is a privilege to be called to go first even when it means you are the first to suffer and the only one at risk. It means you must bear the weight of responsibility and accept the consequences that will come with the privilege.

Whenever God moves forward, it is in conflict with many other forces. The kingdom of God can expand only out of conflict with the kingdom of darkness. Hate does not surrender easily to love, nor does evil submit quietly to good. When you seize divine moments, there is a spiritual collision, and a part of seizing those moments to the fullest is a willingness to bear the initial impact alone.

Almost weekly people from around the world come to Mosaic, often not simply to experience the community and celebration of Mosaic, but also to see how we "do church." It is inevitable that we are asked what have we done to see a church like Mosaic flourish. Most of the inquiries, though well motivated, are about church growth. The nutshell question is, "What did you do to get the church growing?" Before I even begin to attempt to answer that question, I have my own question that I like to ask: "Are you willing to do the right things even if the result is decline?" I then explain why this is a critical question. We are doing the same things now that we are growing that we were doing when we were declining.

At one point it would have been fair to describe our condition as hemorrhaging. It felt very much like one of those scenes from *ER* where you begin to squirm as they cut through the chest, then saw through the ribs to get to the heart. At first description, it sounds like an act of abuse, but once you understand it, you realize it is an act of mercy and intervention.

It was a Saturday morning, and I received an abrupt phone call from one of our elders. Almost immediately into the conversation Robert said something that any pastor would dread: "Erwin, the elders decided to meet without you, and I was selected to call you and tell you the outcome of our meeting." I could feel my entire body reacting to his statement. Things had been pretty tough, and it looked as though they were about to get worse.

As much as I admired the men who served as elders, the former pastor had selected them all. His tenure had lasted nearly twenty-five years, and he had remained as a part of the eldership for more than five years into my role as lead pastor. What for a season was a private disagreement had grown to public division. His departure had deeply wounded our community of faith and took a huge toll on all of us. I knew that I would not make it through unscarred, but I didn't know whether I would make it through. I would not have blamed the elders if they had met for the purpose of asking me for my resignation. And then I heard his words, "Enrique, Rick, and I have met, and we want you to know if there are only our three families who are left, we are with you. Do not turn back, do not back down, because what you are doing is right."

That phone call was like fresh wind to my sail. It was God strengthening the magnetic force of due north. I had a group of men around me who were more committed to doing what was right than doing what was easy. They believed that our suffering would be rewarded by God's approval. Everything didn't get better after this conversation. In fact, the conflicts that we faced only accelerated. For six months the weight of my responsibility not only affected my physical health, but also brought great pain to my family. One of the small reminders that even when I felt that I was doing okay I was damaged goods was the twitch in my right eye.

I often wondered whether I would make it through and find the health that I had known before this season in my life, yet the memories of what we went through only add to the incredible joy and fulfillment we experience today. I can't even imagine leaving Mosaic. The fact that we stayed during the worst of times only reinforces that I'm not about to leave during the best of times. This doesn't mean that everything is easy, but there are very few things like the initial impact when you first engage a battle that must be fought.

Anyone who's ever served as a leader understands the loneliness of the role. There are moments that are not shared with anyone. A part of the calling is to bear the initial impact on the behalf of others. This is true in every meaningful endeavor and was so beautifully modeled by our Lord Jesus Christ. The cross was His place alone. No one else could bear it for us. From Gethsemane to Calvary, Jesus chose the lonely place. Even His cry to the Father, "My God, My God, why have You forsaken Me?" reminds us that God allows us to go to places where the weight of desperation presses against our hearts.

ANYONE WHO'S EVER SERVED AS A LEADER UNDERSTANDS THE LONELINESS OF THE ROLE. THERE ARE MOMENTS THAT ARE NOT SHARED WITH ANYONE.

Those men and women whom God uses to write the pages of history understand the depth of this principle, that God paves the way through the willing sacrifice of individuals. Through these individuals God makes known to all who will listen what is on His heart.

One of my team members and I took an exploratory trip to various overseas locations. The journey took us to India, Pakistan, Cambodia, China, Hong Kong, and finally Japan. On the last leg of our travels we were in the Shabuya District of Tokyo. It was one of the busiest intersections I had ever seen. The traffic of business executives moving through the crowded intersection was almost overwhelming. There was a strange contradiction between the clean and professional environment in which we stood and the sex hotels that were not very far away. I had always understood Japan to be essentially without religion, so what transpired caught me off guard.

A small army of evangelists descended on the crowd. They were everywhere in every direction, walking up to businessmen and women and asking them if they could pray for them. Quickly one approached us and asked in fluent English if he could pray for us too. I asked him to whom they were praying. He avoided the question and asked again if he could pray for us. This time I offered to pray for him and explained to him that I would pray to the living God whose name is Jesus. I soon learned they were a part of a cult that was headquartered in Pasadena, California. They were well aware of the spiritual emptiness among the Japanese people. The leader of their movement seemed to know that American influence passed on capitalism, but failed to pass on the Christian faith.

But there was one bright light in the midst of all of this commotion. Our guide that evening was a young Japanese woman we will call Yoshiko. She was a genuine follower of Jesus Christ. Her burden for reaching her own people with the love of God was both moving and convicting. For some reason she seemed encouraged that we had come to Tokyo to bring some small support and help. Her prayer was so simple and transparent. As she wept she confessed to God, "I thought I was all alone." Somehow just knowing someone else was there seemed a great gift to her. She seemed fragile and powerful in that moment. An honest confession of the pain of living in the lonely place and an unshakable determination to bring her nation to Christ even if she was alone.

Divine moments abound for those who are willing to bear the initial impact. Often alone when it comes to men, never alone when it comes to God.

THEY INCARNATE THE HEART OF GOD

This might have been Jonathan's greatest contribution. Through his actions, he personified what was on God's mind and what was on God's heart. He became a personal testament of the values and directions that God's people should express. It was as if God put flesh and blood on His purpose and his name was Jonathan. If you wanted to know what God was doing, you could just look at him.

Whenever we seize divine moments, we magnify the presence of God. To act on God's behalf is to express what's on His mind and on His heart. When we do this, we become a flagship of God's activity. It is the contemporary equivalent of the pagans who called the followers of Christ Christians because they looked like Jesus. They moved in a divine rhythm. To watch a follower of Christ live was to see God move. They were not carbon copies of Jesus, but dynamic expressions of His character. And when things got tough, the image of Christ in them became clear. No matter how dark darkness is, it is never thick enough to snuff out the light.

THEY WERE NOT CARBON COPIES OF JESUS, BUT DYNAMIC EXPRESSIONS OF HIS CHARACTER.

When Kim and I were preparing to get married, we had only one car between the two of us. It was her old Ford Pinto. I went to the airport to pick up my brother in her car, and the Pinto died at the terminal. My wife loved her first car, and so we mercifully put her Pinto to sleep. Soon a friend of ours called us and offered us several thousand dollars to buy a car. He told us he felt God had instructed him to provide this gift for us. We stopped at one particular car dealership and began talking with a salesman named Dan.

In many ways the conversation was a comedy. He kept trying to get the hard facts, such as income, amount of down payment, what monthly payments we could afford. We kept explaining to him that we were in school, had no money, had no idea what our future income was, but that God always provided for us and was doing so again. It was an opportunity to share our life in Christ with this man whose whole goal was to sell us this car.

That night when I returned to my dorm, there was a note taped to the door. As I opened it, I realized it was from the salesman at the car dealership. It was a desperate note, a cry for help. I'll never forget how he began that letter: "I don't know why I'm here or why I'm writing this note. I just got the feeling that maybe you could help."

I gave him a call and began a series of conversations with him and his wife. I discovered he had been a professional draftsman who had lost his job. In frustration, anger, and desperation, he committed arson against the company that had dismissed him. He was found out and spent time in prison. Now he was trying to provide for his family by selling cars. It was basically the only job he could get.

It was Christmas Eve when I sat in their home and knelt with Dan and his wife, and in brokenness both received Jesus Christ as their Lord and God. It was our privilege to minister to them for several months afterward and to know that in the end he was able to return to his original profession.

WHEN WE OFFER OURSELVES AS INSTRUMENTS FOR GOD'S PURPOSE, WE CREATE OPPORTUNITIES FOR OTHERS TO EXPERIENCE GOD THROUGH US.

Dan is a good reminder that what looks like a routine encounter from one end could have all the markings of a divine moment on the other. And it really wasn't that I seized that moment, but that that moment seized me. I stepped into that moment, but I never foresaw the outcome. Dan's earnestness to find me reminds me that people are looking for God. When we offer ourselves as instruments for God's purpose, we create opportunities for others to experience God through us. We become living lightning rods of

God's activity. Our lives become the X that marks the spot. Our obedience creates a spiritual epicenter through which God shakes up the world around us and others come to know Him.

HIS KINGDOM COME

While our actions illuminate what God is doing, divine moments create an opportunity for even more than that. It is when we are seizing divine moments that we are best positioned to see God work in an undeniable way. While Jonathan was at war fighting with all of his strength, using all of his skill, God did more. God shook the earth. He sent the panic throughout the camp. He made sure that no one could miss that moment. He let everyone know that Jonathan was not alone, but that God was involved. God loves affirming His purpose and, even more so, His people when they embrace His purpose.

Up to now you might say that Jonathan moved without God, but God clearly redirects our thinking. God was without question in that moment. I think it's safe to say that God was thrilled to affirm and support Jonathan's action. God just loves it when someone does the right thing regardless of personal consequence. When we are doing His will and therefore have ensured our failure unless He intervenes, it is His perfect context.

We can never ultimately fulfill God's purpose for our lives without Him, yet we will never know God's power until we begin to move in His purpose. There may not be anything more thrilling than embracing the God-given opportunity, knowing you're in over your head and then watching God come through. While this journey will often ensure that you will bear the initial impact alone and while you can find satisfaction in knowing that your life has expressed the mind and heart of God, there is nothing that compares to that moment when God's hand becomes undeniable and He makes visible the invisible. It is very much as if God is highlighting His most urgent agendas for our lives. Time and again I have been amazed at how God has taken our work that was done in obscurity and highlighted it for His purpose.

It was about fifteen years ago when our small work in south Dallas seemed to be getting an inordinate amount of attention. Though we were small, we were watching God use us to make a much bigger impact. The influence of Cornerstone seemed to be growing disproportionately to our size. Both the national and the international mission boards of our denomination decided to use our work as a primary focus for a short film they were making, giving attention to our cooperative program for missions. That weekend they sent a film crew to follow me through our concrete jungle and capture the work that was being done.

On Sunday morning the process was pretty simple. They set their film crew up outside the church facility, and during the morning service, different interviews were scheduled with various attenders at our gathering. While they were safely outside, we were experiencing something quite different on the inside.

A tall and slender man wearing black leather walked into the church building and demanded to speak to the pastor. Our associate pastor took him into my office and sent someone to grab me from the auditorium. It was almost 11:00 A.M., and our service was about to begin, so I knew I had only a few moments. As the three of us sat in that room, he began to explain to me that voices told him to stop me from preaching the gospel of Jesus Christ. He took a knife from his jacket and placed it on my desk and said I could hold it so that I wouldn't worry about him hurting me. I wasn't really worried about the knife. In retrospect I think it would have been far more important for him to give me the gun strapped to his leg.

As he explained to me that his life was one of wandering the streets, obeying the voices that spoke to him in his head, I calmly looked at this man named John, and I said, "Sir, if you're hearing voices, it is most likely one of two things. You need psychiatric help, or you're demon possessed." He didn't seem at all offended that I was telling him he was potentially crazy, but the demon-possessed part seemed to really get to him.

He looked at my associate David, who was sitting next to him, and said, "Did he say demon possessed?" David simply nodded yes. This man looked at me, and I cannot explain what I heard. I can only tell you that from the best of my perception I heard multiple voices coming out of this man at one time, and they said, "Would you like to call us out by name?"

I could not remember one single seminary class that prepared me for that moment. My degree in psychology from the University of North Carolina didn't seem very helpful at that moment either. I wish I could tell you that my response was either profound or courageous, but I said, "No, I just want to talk to John." I quickly offered to pray for him.

He stood in anger, and he said, "No, let me pray for you."

I said, "Okay. You pray to your god, and then I'll pray to mine."

In anger he rushed out of the room. I thought he left the building. I ran to the nursery to make sure he didn't go to the children. He had, in fact, gone straight into the sanctuary, walked up the aisle, stepped up to the podium, and began calling everyone to attention. Someone ran to the back and grabbed me and told me what was happening. I walked into the auditorium, strode down the center aisle, and commanded him in the name of Jesus to come down.

I've always wondered what Jesus meant when He said, "Whatever you ask in My name, I will do it." I always felt uncomfortable with people who would pray in Jesus' name and just assume it would happen because of the tagline. The phrase seemed to me a Christian cliché or, maybe better yet, an incantation or a mantra. It's as if saying "in Jesus' name" will do the trick. That moment clarified more theology than hours of classroom time. When Jesus said there is power in praying in His name, He was implying something deeper than a confession.

In that moment I knew I was doing what Jesus would do. I had a clear sense that I was expressing what was on His mind and in His heart. I had the authority of His name because I was moving where He was moving. As I walked closer and closer to the podium, I kept repeating, "In the name of Jesus I command you to come down."

After the third or fourth time, he stopped his ranting. He became quiet, stepped down from the podium, and fell down on the floor to his knees with his face to the ground.

Next to him was our associate pastor David, who had been with me in the room. He explained to me later that John looked at him and said, "Do you want to know what I'm praying?" David said, "No," and it angered him. And so he asked him again, "Do you want to know what I'm praying?" And David said, "Yes." He said, "I'm praying that those people will stop following that man, that those sheep will stop following that shepherd."

Then he rose to his feet, and he asked me my name. I told him it was Erwin. He started screaming my name, and then he looked at me with a clear threat and said, "I'll be back, Erwin."

I looked at him and said, "And I'll be here."

With that he stormed out of the doors, turned to his right, turned to his right again, and accidentally walked to where the film crews were. They assumed he was the next member to be interviewed, and we have him on film. They asked him the same question they asked others, "What is the number one problem facing south Dallas?" Ready for his answer, they were caught off guard when he bluntly stated, "The white man." They regrouped and asked him to name another problem. And this answer was far more intriguing. He said, "You've got the needy and the greedy, a place full of need and greed." He went on to explain the real challenge is to be able to distinguish between the two.

John became a part of our cooperative program mission effort. It was almost as if God, with His unique sense of humor, wanted us all to know there is more going on than meets the eye. I'm convinced this was one of those divine moments with multiple levels. God was making sure we filmed more than what the church was doing. He wanted to make sure we had a deeper sense of what He was doing through the church. There was real spiritual warfare taking place, real human beings captive to the power of darkness, real danger lurking not only in shadows, but in the hearts of men. Yes, God wanted a record not of a nice little ministry among the urban poor, but of a war that was raging where the souls of men, women, and children were at stake.

When Jesus was teaching His disciples how to pray, He instructed them to pray these words: "Your kingdom come, your will be done on earth as it is in heaven" (Matt. 6:10). Divine moments contain the power to usher in the kingdom of God. When we choose to live our lives in such a way that His will is done on earth as it is in heaven, the kingdom of God prevails over the kingdom of darkness. Whenever we are willing to bear the initial impact, whenever we choose to seize those divine moments whatever the cost, we create the opportunity for God to make visible the invisible, for God to shake things up, for God to make

Himself known. When we seize divine moments, we mark the epicenter of God's activity. When we choose to live a life bigger than ourselves, God uses us to shake things up.

The battle raged from one place and time to another. The enemy held such unfair advantage. He knew every fear, every doubt, every weakness they held. He would choose the battleground and then change it when it was to his favor.

Ayden and Kembr stood shoulder to shoulder as they fought back the endless darkness. The light served them as sickles cutting through the shadows.

Their shrieks would expose them as they moved with force toward Ayden and Kembr. The shadows knew if they could divide the two, it would cause them to weaken and perhaps fall back.

"We are almost to the darkest place," Ayden exhorted as they fought their way forward. It was there that Maven told him the light would find its highest density.

They all heard the distant rumblings. Then like the most glorious of sunrises, light appeared that was so expansive, it marked the horizon.

"Look," Ayden shouted. "The light pursues us!"

— Entry 2358
The Perils of Ayden

8

MOVEMENT

IGNITE A REACTION

I HAD BEEN INVITED TO LEAD A DISCIPLESHIP WEEKEND for young professionals who worked in the nation's capital. Washington, D.C., is a magnet for young, aggressive, and ambitious professionals. The focus of this weekend retreat was evangelism and how to invest your life in the lives of others for the purpose of bringing them to Christ. I was brimming with excitement as I thought about the potential, gifting, and influence that would be locked away in this conference. The setting was beautiful—everything I would expect for this kind of audience. Surrounded with a lake, an endless forest of trees, the serenity that only urban professionals can afford.

My assessment was that the weekend went well. They seemed more than attentive; they seemed genuinely engaged in the content. I was so inspired that I made an offer to extend the learning experience. I suggested that we meet back in Washington and take what we learned and apply it together. We set a time to meet at the Capitol Hill Metropolitan Baptist Church. I was sure that I would be greeted with a throng of eager learners. I was destined to be disappointed. In short, I was stood up. The group might have been moved, but they certainly were not mobilized.

But the evening was not a complete loss. That same weekend one of the professionals who worked at the White House had invited me on a private tour of the president's home. While no one showed up when it was time to apply the learning of our weekend seminar, a small but eager group arrived an hour later because they heard I had received this invitation to go to the White House. President Reagan had a national speech to deliver that day, so late into the evening the two of us, plus the handful who crashed our presidential tour, headed to the White House. The tour was to take place about an hour after my failed evangelism training opportunity. And then the scariest thing happened. There was no small discomfort as they sheepishly explained why they couldn't make it to the first appointment, but were early for the second.

They rejected the first invitation and came to the second without invitation. It seems that most of us would rather see the president than see God or, in this case, see where the president works rather than see God work. And so off we went to see the Oval Office and to step into the center of global power.

There was just one thing I didn't tell them. I moved the evangelism experience back an hour and slightly altered the location. I was clear this was our divine moment. You really can't schedule God anyway. So the night workers at the White House became our first opportunity to share our faith. Though my conversations were limited, at least they saw that I made an effort. But what happened afterward was even more interesting.

It was nearly three o'clock in the morning, and since I had never seen the Jefferson Memorial, they agreed to drive by this beautiful tribute to freedom and genius. As we walked down the stairs, we saw a cluster of young urban professionals sipping champagne on the steps of the memorial. One of the professionals with me saw the group and eagerly prodded me to go and talk to them. I responded, "If you think we're supposed to talk to them, then you go talk to them." He refused, and I said I wouldn't do what God had just told him to do. After all, he was the one who noted the opportunity. He clearly felt prompted to speak with them. It was obvious that it wasn't a lack of desire that held him back, but fear. Over the years, I have learned to recognize that this kind of prompting is God's Spirit speaking to us. I was hoping that my refusal to go in his place would instigate him to seize his divine moment.

And then I heard the shout, "Hey, you!" At first I didn't know where it was coming from. Then I heard it again: "Hey, you!"

I turned and said, "Excuse me?"

He said, "It's not 'excuse me.' It's 'God bless you' that you're supposed to say."

I was a bit confused.

He explained, "When a person sneezes, you're supposed to say, 'God bless you.'"

He did not say, "Hey, you!" It was "ah-choo." He had sneezed, not shouted. Nevertheless the conversation had begun.

After he explained to me the correct response to a sneeze, I looked at him and said, "Well, God can bless you if you want Him to."

He said, "Sure, come and tell me how God can bless me."

And at three o'clock in the morning on the steps of the Jefferson Memorial we seized another divine moment. I'll never forget how these powerful, aggressive professionals lined up behind me like little ducklings following their mother, both intimidated and exhilarated as we entered the moment.

We approached the small group of D.C. professionals, not unlike the group standing right behind me. They were cordial and friendly and seemed eager to engage in conversation. As I began to explain to them how God could bless them through the person of Jesus Christ, the young exec positioned in the middle of the group was more than irritated when he discovered I was a Christian. I picked this up from a comment he made. It went something like this: "Oh, no, you're a Christian. You know what I hate about Christians?" Years of training have given me the keen skill to be able to read between the lines. I quickly concluded this guy hates Christians. And since I'm a Christian, he suddenly hates me.

Not really sure I wanted to know the answer, I went ahead and prompted his response: "What is it you hate about Christians?"

He stated, "You Christians live by faith."

I asked him, "What do you live by?"

He sneered back (he really did sneer), "I live by reason."

I asked him, "Whose reason do you live by?" We had spent time talking about Locke, Hume, Descartes, and other philosophers. So I continued. "Do you live by Locke's reason? Or Hume's reason?" Then pointing to those with him, "Or by the reason of your friends? Whose reason do you live by?"

He answered without hesitation, "My reason."

Then I asked, "How do you know your reason is right?"

There was a moment of silent meditation. I'm pretty sure there was no prayer involved since he didn't believe in God. But finally he broke the silence. In a voice that sounded pained in its expression, he said, "By faith."

At that point everyone could see we both lived by faith.

So I asked him one final question: "I've chosen to put my faith in Jesus Christ, who was crucified and then rose from the dead. You have chosen to put your faith in yourself. I know what Jesus has done. What exactly have you done lately?" I admit maybe a different approach would have been better, but I was in the moment and it just seemed the right thing to say. I will say the response of his friends was very positive. A faith built on reason is not a reasonable faith. In the end, we are all required to put our trust in something. For him it was his own intellect. For me it is the person of Jesus Christ. I was grateful that for this small group of seekers faith seemed far more reasonable than rationalism.

One of the great privileges God gives us is that of bringing others into His activity. Whenever we choose to engage a divine opportunity, there is the real potential of bringing others into God's presence and God's purpose. God uses those men and women who choose to live on the front lines to draw His people into the battle.

WHENEVER WE CHOOSE TO ENGAGE A DIVINE OPPORTUNITY, THERE IS THE REAL POTENTIAL OF BRINGING OTHERS INTO GOD'S PRESENCE AND GOD'S PURPOSE.

Samuel told us that after the earthquake,

> Saul's lookouts at Gibeah in Benjamin saw the army melting away in all directions. Then Saul said to the men who were with him, "Muster the forces and see who has left us." When they did, it was Jonathan and his armor-bearer who were not there.
>
> Saul said to Ahijah, "Bring the ark of God." (At that time it was with the Israelites.) While Saul was talking to the priest, the tumult in the Philistine camp increased more and more. So Saul said to the priest, "Withdraw your hand." (1 Sam. 14:16–19)

Jonathan did not have time or inclination to draw attention to himself. He wasn't trying to market himself or ensure that everybody knew what he was doing. He was focused on the task. He was in the middle of the battle. He was at war. He had no time to think of himself, no time to think through how to capitalize on his venture. In that moment he was just doing what was right. God was the One who raised the awareness of Jonathan's actions. There was no need for self-promotion. But without question, God wanted to promote what Jonathan was doing.

The lookouts of Israel saw what was happening, what they

could describe only as the army of the Philistines melting away in every direction. Saul instinctively knew that one among them had to be the catalyst of the event. It should not surprise us that when God is moving, there is a human agent of change. When He pulled the army together, there was only one soldier who was doing what soldiers are supposed to do. The rest had been sleeping. It was Jonathan who was at war.

Then Saul did what would seem to be the most spiritual thing. He called the priest of God to bring the ark of God so that they could pray and seek the Lord. After all, how can you act without knowing God's will? But there was too much commotion for a meaningful time of prayer. While Saul was talking to the priest, the tumult in the Philistine camp increased more and more. And so Saul said to the priest, "Withdraw your hand." Best modern translation: *There's no time for praying now.*

LEFT STANDING AT THE ALTAR

Have you ever felt that you were always one step behind? That you keep trying to seize a divine moment one moment too late? Ever live the nightmare that the starting gun has shot and you're still sitting in the blocks? It was more than a nightmare for me; it was a reality.

It was an AAU track-and-field event in Miami, Florida. I was only in junior high, and the surroundings of a university sports arena were more than intimidating. I was to run the 400 meters as my primary event. It was clear as I measured the strength of my competition that they were all superior athletes and I was way out of my league. I knew my only hope to compete well in the event was to get an extraordinary start. You get two false starts in track, and I already had one. I knew if I jumped the gun again, I would be disqualified from the race. I desired to get out early, but the rush of adrenaline got me in trouble the first time. So I waited, knowing I had no room for error. I can't even explain what happened. It all happened so fast. Well, it happened fast for everyone else—slow for me. The gun went off, everyone moved, and I was paralyzed in the blocks. By the time I left I was far too late. I had left first the first time out and finished last the second time out.

That was Saul. He was acting when he should have been waiting; he was controlling when he should have been praying; he was sleeping when he should have been fighting; and there he was again, praying when he should have been moving. He just couldn't get it right. Yet when you break the situation down, it was never because things were unclear. God continuously told him what to do. Saul knew that even though he was king, only Samuel was authorized to make the offering before the Lord. Samuel had instructed Saul to wait seven days for his arrival. When Samuel did not arrive early enough on that seventh day, Saul took things into his own hands. When Samuel arrived, he rebuked Saul not for acting out of ignorance, but for disobeying what God had commanded him to do.

THAT WAS SAUL. HE WAS ACTING WHEN HE SHOULD HAVE BEEN WAITING; HE WAS CONTROLLING WHEN HE SHOULD HAVE BEEN PRAYING; HE WAS SLEEPING WHEN HE SHOULD HAVE BEEN FIGHTING; AND THERE HE WAS AGAIN, PRAYING WHEN HE SHOULD HAVE BEEN MOVING.

Saul knew to wait on Samuel, but he didn't. He knew to go to war, but he didn't. It wasn't because God's will was so difficult to understand that he kept missing his divine moments. It was simply because he chose not to trust God and act on His word. Don't miss the point: God has not remained silent. He has spoken both through the Word, who has walked among us, and through His Word that He has written to guide us. The adventure begins here. Live out what God has already spoken, and you will not find God silent.

What Saul did next was very religious. On the surface it appeared to be deeply spiritual. He called the priest of God and the ark of God and began the process of asking God what to do. It is obviously essential to seek God's face, to take time to enter God's presence, to be transformed by who He is. To live a prayerless life is to miss the life that God created you to experience. Yet there are times when prayer can become a religious veil for an empty life.

> **TO LIVE A PRAYERLESS LIFE IS TO MISS THE LIFE THAT GOD CREATED YOU TO EXPERIENCE. YET THERE ARE TIMES WHEN PRAYER CAN BECOME A RELIGIOUS VEIL FOR AN EMPTY LIFE.**

Jesus warned us of this. He told us specifically not to pray as the pagans do. He was referring to the practice of meaningless repetition in prayer. For some reason we can't shake free from a view that God is impressed with how much we pray.

I remember my first confession during my catechism. The process is simple: you step into the confessional; you tell the priest all the sins you can think of; he gives you the appropriate prayer assignment so that your sins can be forgiven. I balked. I just couldn't tell the priest my deepest, darkest secrets. I'm sure he would have been shocked by the nefarious life of a ten-year-old. But finally I coughed it up. I confessed that in my anger I had called Jesus stupid. Looking back, I don't know that that was what really made him mad. It was my earlier claim to sinlessness. I had insisted I didn't have any sins. And while he recommended certain sins to reflect upon, I kept assuring him that I had never done any of those. After the confession about Jesus, I was holding to sinless perfection. How could I be certain this priest would not shortly be having a conversation with my mom?

Then came my penance. I don't remember the exact numbers, but my recollection is pretty close. He assigned me nearly two hundred "Our Fathers" and more than three hundred "Acts of Contrition." I guess the theory goes like this: the more sin you have, the more you better pray. I was obviously in deep trouble with the Deity. I wasn't about to tell the priest I had never memorized the Acts of Contrition. I had faked my way through catechism.

So I solemnly walked to the front of the altar. People kneeling throughout the cathedral were praying their countless prayers. I knelt with all of the reverence I knew how to muster, and it began by negotiation. I said, "God, I don't know the Acts of Contrition, so I can't pray any of those. I do know the Our Father, but I just can't see the purpose of praying it again and again. So I'm going to pray it three times: once for You, Father; once for the Holy Spirit; and once for Jesus; and I hope that will be enough."

Even then I just couldn't see how God would be moved through redundancy. It's almost as if we think God keeps a tabulation of the number of words we offer up in prayer. Jesus said, "When you pray, do not keep on babbling like pagans, for they think they will be heard because of their many words. Do not be like them, for your Father knows what you need before you ask him" (Matt. 6:7–8).

IF ONE DANGER IN REGARD TO PRAYER IS TO BE PRAYERLESS, ANOTHER IS TO PRAY MORE AND REMAIN EMPTY OF GENUINE CONTACT WITH GOD.

Too much of our literature regarding prayer is overfocused on *how much* we pray and too little focused on what happens *when* we pray. If one danger in regard to prayer is to be prayerless, another is to pray more and remain empty of genuine contact with God.

Jesus attacked the framework that believes we will be heard because of our many words. He even implied that it is the result of an improper view of God. He said, "Do not be like them because your Father knows what you need before you ask Him."

Prayer is not about informing God of your needs, nor is it even about trying to convince God to help you. Prayer is about connecting to God. It is about experiencing His presence and moving with Him in intimate communion. Jesus reminded us that God is not callous to our needs. Many times our view on prayer implies that God is unconcerned or apathetic. He gives us the imagery. He contrasted God the Father to the man who refuses to get up to provide bread for a friend, but relents because of the other man's perseverance. God is eager to give us both His gifts and Himself if we will ask Him, yet there is an even greater and more subtle danger in the arena of prayer. It is when prayer is reactive rather than proactive. It is the way we subtly use prayer not to seek God's will, but to delay our obedience to His will.

PRAYER IS NOT ABOUT INFORMING GOD OF YOUR NEEDS, NOR IS IT EVEN ABOUT TRYING TO CONVINCE GOD TO HELP YOU. PRAYER IS ABOUT CONNECTING TO GOD. IT IS ABOUT EXPERIENCING HIS PRESENCE AND MOVING WITH HIM IN INTIMATE COMMUNION.

While Saul was praying, Jonathan was obeying. While Saul was trying to figure out the will of God, Jonathan was busy working out the will of God. I cannot count the number of times I have given counsel to individuals who seemed unable to discern what was the right thing to do. You would think those situations were highly complex and difficult to unravel, yet most of the time the counsel I gave was not the result of high discernment or unique intuition. Their situation was so clearly defined in the Scriptures that there was no ambiguity about what they should do. Too often the response was the same: "I need to pray about it."

A young follower of Christ in a destructive dating relationship is unwilling to end it even when she knows she should not be involved with someone who has not embraced the values and heart of God.

A husband whose business "belongs to God" is working virtually 24/7 while his marriage is falling apart and his children are going astray.

A deacon or financial chairman begins coalescing a mob of inactive members from his church in order to fire their new pastor.

A young couple living together are convinced that being in love overrides the biblical call not to have sex until after they're married.

It may be hard to believe, but in these circumstances and many others, the response of people who consider themselves sincere Christians is, "I need to pray about it."

THE **OBSTACLE** OF **PRAYER**

Prayer can be a religious form of rebellion. While feigning a need to get clarity from God, we are actually avoiding what God has made clear. We don't like what the Scriptures say. What Jesus is calling us to do is different from what we want to do. How God desires for us to respond conflicts with how we want to respond. Even though the instructions are clear, even though the will of God is written without ambiguity, we feign obedience by claiming a need to seek God in prayer. There are some things we just don't need to pray about. While many things in life remain a mystery, there are some things that God has spoken clearly. Here what we need to do is not pray, but obey. And let's be honest, sometimes obeying is a lot harder than praying.

When we pray about things already decided, we are wasting our time and missing divine moments. At the same time, we are not positioned to seize divine moments when we neglect to pray. Prayer keeps you in step with God's Spirit and in tune to His voice. If you are living a prayerless life, then you must heed the call of the apostle Paul to pray without ceasing. Our lives are to be a continuous conversation with God. This kind of life of prayer is one where we are sensitive to every prompting and whisper of God. We are not only informing God, but God is informing us. He is an active and intimate participant in our daily choices.

WE ARE NOT POSITIONED TO SEIZE DIVINE MOMENTS WHEN WE NEGLECT TO PRAY.

Prayer is an obstacle when we keep praying about things of which God has already spoken. If He has commanded us in His Word, there is nothing to pray about—just obey.

Prayer can also be an obstacle when we hide behind prayer while the moment needs action. There are moments when it is too late for praying. It is when God has already spoken and we are late to the appointment. When that's the case, we need to run.

We don't need to pray about loving. We are already commanded to love. We don't need to pray about forgiving. We are already commanded to forgive. We don't need to pray about being in community or confessing our faith. Neither do we need to pray about whether we should be arrogant or humble, takers or givers, indulgers or servers. God has already spoken on all these issues and more. When you do pray on these matters, God confirms what He has said with the added element of *What are you waiting for?*

Saul was praying when he should have been obeying. Is it possible that we are committing the same sin? Are you using prayer as a way of resisting God's will rather than as a way of accessing God's will? Jesus did not have a value for prayer for prayer's sake. He had a value for the intimate communion between God and man.

JESUS DID NOT HAVE A VALUE FOR PRAYER FOR PRAYER'S SAKE. HE HAD A VALUE FOR THE INTIMATE COMMUNION BETWEEN GOD AND MAN.

The purpose of prayer is to know God and, in knowing Him, to hear God's voice and understand that God has heard your voice. The end result of this kind of prayer is a heart pliable enough to move wherever God is calling.

The purpose of prayer is to keep you connected, and when you're connected to God, you are moving with Him. Prayer that connects you to God positions you to seize divine moments. This kind of prayer gives you the courage to live the life of an adventurer. Prayer should move you, not paralyze you. And when you pray with intent to obey, you become a magnet who draws others into God's presence. You can choose to establish a monument for prayer or pray to unleash a movement. One is religious; the other revolutionary.

In 1 Kings 18 we step into one of history's most unique prayer meetings: Elijah versus the prophets of Baal. If you examine the passage carefully, you will find that the prophets of Baal by far exceeded Elijah in both time and effort in prayer. Two altars were established. The prophets and Elijah were to pray to their deity or deities and invoke them to send fire from heaven, and whichever deity answered, all those who were in attendance would then conclude that He was the one, true God.

The prophets of Baal prayed from morning until noon: "'O Baal, answer us!' they shouted. But there was no response; no one answered. And they danced around the altar they had made" (1 Kings 18:26). About noon Elijah began to taunt them:

> "Shout louder!" he said. "Surely he is a god! Perhaps he is deep in thought, or busy, or traveling. Maybe he is sleeping and must be awakened." So they shouted louder and slashed themselves with swords and spears, as was their custom, until their blood flowed. Midday passed, and they continued their frantic prophesying until the time for the evening sacrifice. But there was no response, no one answered, no one paid attention. (1 Kings 18:27–29)

They prayed long and hard. One small problem, they were praying to no god at all. It's a terrible thing when you waste a life of prayer on the wrong god.

Elijah, on the other hand, prayed a very brief prayer: "O LORD, God of Abraham, Isaac and Israel, let it be known today that you are God in Israel and that I am your servant and have done all these things at your command. Answer me, O LORD, answer me, so these people will know that you, O LORD, are God, and that you are turning their hearts back again" (1 Kings 18:36–37). End of prayer.

The Scriptures describe what happened in that moment: "Then the fire of the LORD fell and burned up the sacrifice, the wood, the stones and the soil, and also licked up the water in the trench. When all the people saw this, they fell prostrate and cried, 'The LORD—he is God! The LORD—he is God!'" (vv. 38–39).

The truth of the matter is that around the world people pray, and there are endless numbers of religions where people pray both earnestly and incessantly. Some pray five times a day facing east; others have escaped the noisiness of the real world and have locked themselves away in caves or castles that they may only pray. I do not believe that God calls any one of us to a life of prayer that forever isolates us from the world around us. The same God who calls us to meet Him in the solitude of a lonely place also commissions us to return to the crowded streets where people desperately need a touch from God. Elijah gave us tremendous insight to the very purpose of prayer: "Answer me, Lord, so that everyone can know that You are God and that I am Your servant simply doing what You have commanded me."

WHEN WE OBEY AND THEN PRAY, WE ACKNOWLEDGE THAT GOD HAS INITIATED THE RELATIONSHIP WITH US.

Small prayers have huge impact when they come from people who are living a life of obedience to God. He wasn't praying and then obeying. He was obeying and then praying. When we pray before we obey, we imply that we're the initiators of the relationship with God. When we obey and then pray, we acknowledge that God has initiated the relationship with us. God has spoken. He sent the first word. Our first response is to hear His voice and move in alignment to His commands. Out of that obedience our intimacy with Him grows, and then when we speak to Him, He answers us and makes Himself known.

In all of his errors, there was one thing that Saul got right. When the battle around him became too loud for Saul to pray, he recognized that there was no time for praying. It was time to obey. God was already clearly at work. He needed to mobilize the people of God and get in on what God was doing.

I am reminded of Samuel's question to Saul at a later time: "Why did you not obey the LORD?" And Samuel's reminder to him: "Does the LORD delight in burnt offerings and sacrifices as much as in obeying the voice of the LORD? To obey is better than sacrifice, and to heed is better than the fat of rams" (1 Sam. 15:19, 22).

There are moments when our obedience is to stop and pray,

and in those moments comes the word that we must *go* and *obey*. And it is in this obedience that the voice of God becomes intimately clear.

PRAYING IN THE FOXHOLE

We had just moved to Los Angeles and were serving as volunteers at The Church on Brady. We had lived in the Dallas-Fort Worth metroplex for nearly ten years. Kim and I both finished our master's degrees and remained in the region working with urban poor people. During that time I began working for the North American Mission Board as a metropolitan evangelism consultant. At the end of a three-year term, we determined to move to Los Angeles for the next phase of our ministry. The Church on Brady seemed a perfect fit to serve as our base of ministry. Knowing that my work required an immense amount of travel, I wanted to make sure we were part of a community of faith that would become an extended family to us. We were still working through the process of an entire reorganization of our life, ministry, and finances. During that time the church had graciously offered to carry our insurance, yet somehow in the process our paperwork was misplaced. Without knowing it, we were uninsured for about a year.

My wife, Kim, in all of our years of marriage, had never been sick. I used to say that she had a perfect record of health except for the two times she had to go to the hospital. But she politely reminded me that being pregnant and having a baby was not a sickness. So if you eliminate the two deliveries, Kim had a record of perfect health.

Well, you can almost guess what happened. The best way to remain healthy is to make sure you have insurance. The best way to ensure that you're going to be sick is to have no insurance at all. In the midst of this season, Kim began having debilitating pains in her abdomen. The pain went from severe to unbearable. I watched my wife without any notice move into a fetal position, writhing in anguish. During one of those attacks we rushed her for medical attention, and she was placed in the hospital for several days. They explained to us that she had gallstones, but that three of them had lodged themselves in rather critical areas and that they were even life threatening. The medical bills quickly rose to thousands of dollars, and the surgery that she would need would press it much further.

In the midst of this crisis, by the way, I discovered that our paperwork had been lost, and we were without coverage. Whatever we did, I would have to find a way to pay for the bills myself. It was difficult enough to see my wife in so much pain, and the added danger to her life and the implications, especially for our two small children, seemed overwhelming. And now to know that a serious error had been made and as a result I could not even provide for Kim's medical needs brought me to the end of myself. I had no doubt that we were in the place where God wanted us to be. Kim and I were not tourists; we were on a mission with Christ together. It was one of those moments when the best thing we could do, the only thing we could do, was pray.

I walked into her hospital room with a desperation that would fuel either depression or intercession. James told us in chapter 5, verse 16 that the desperate prayer of a righteous man is powerful and effective. He used Elijah as an example of the promise. Elijah prayed that it would not rain, and it did not rain for three and a half years. And then he prayed about it again, the heavens opened up, and the rain came and replenished the earth. I had an unexplainable confidence that in this moment God's intention was to heal Kim. I laid hands on her, yet did not pray one of those prayers, "Lord, I don't know Your will, but if You would heal Kim, I sure would appreciate it." Instead, I prayed for God's instantaneous healing for my wife. It wasn't as if I were insisting on something that was unexpected, nor was I trying to move God by the power of my faith. It was more as if God had spoken into my spirit and instructed me to pray this prayer that I would see Him work. I can tell you that in that moment God healed my wife. She left the hospital that day. She left without any pain, and she has been free from symptoms for over a decade.

I am clear that God does not always heal and more than clear that all healing is temporary. But I also know that when you obey and then pray, there is unexplainable power. I make this point because Saul is such a powerful distraction. He stopped to pray at the wrong time and for the wrong reasons. There's no record of it in the text, but I cannot imagine that Jonathan was not praying. Not the long-winded prayers of men who lack the urgency of war, but the gritty and earnest prayers of a man who knows the absence of God means his death. There is an old saying that there are no atheists in foxholes. I wonder if it's also true that there are no true believers in bomb shelters.

THERE IS AN OLD SAYING THAT THERE ARE NO ATHEISTS IN FOXHOLES. I WONDER IF IT'S ALSO TRUE THAT THERE ARE NO TRUE BELIEVERS IN BOMB SHELTERS.

When Elijah prayed, fire came from heaven, and everyone knew God was with him. The end result was that the people of God moved to where Elijah was. This same result was true for Jonathan. He moved where God was; God moved where he was. Soon enough God's people moved to where both were. Jonathans draw God's people into the midst of God's activity.

Does this describe your life? Is the activity of God so powerful around you that it compels others to join you? Do you follow Christ with such passion that others are drawn to join the movement of God? Are you a God magnet? Do people watch your life and conclude, "Everywhere she goes, God shows up"? But you know that the more accurate description is that everywhere God goes, you show up. If this isn't you yet, maybe there's a Jonathan waiting for you to join.

MAKING IT PERSONAL

Long before I came to The Church on Brady, the church had adopted seven target nations around the world. These were nations with significant need, and the leadership was committed to serving the peoples of those countries and reaching them with the gospel of Jesus Christ. A few years into the process, one of the elders of the church and his wife developed a burden for the Kurds. They felt an undeniable call to move with their family to focus on the nation of Turkey. There was one small problem; it wasn't one of the seven target nations. In that particular moment it was outside the field of vision or concern that the congregation and its leadership held. There was even a bit of awkwardness that one of the church's leaders would choose to go to a nontargeted nation. But when asked about this tension, Chris and Karen said simply that they knew God was calling them. There was never a desire to stand against or rebel against spiritual leadership, just an unshakable call to serve the Kurds.

As a result of their act of obedience and their ministry of building shelters for the persecuted people, a unique heart for the Kurds was born in our community. Since that time the church's focus on seven nations has expanded to encompass the whole world. Four families from our Los Angeles community now live in Turkey, and several teams have served in short-term projects. We even went as far as partnering to open a café in the heart of Istanbul. I'm not at liberty to share the details of this amazing place except to say that it is a hip LA-themed hangout where people come together for life-changing dialogue.

One of the wonderful results of seizing a divine moment is that it pulls so many others into theirs. Not everyone moves at the same pace. Some people move at the speed of light, but for some people the light never seems to turn green. What you may never see is the number of people who are pulled into God's purpose for their lives through the wind shear of your obedience.

When Samuel informed us that Saul and all of his men assembled and went to the battle, he was describing a dramatic shift in protocol. The warrior-king was following his son. His reluctance to engage in warfare became an abdication of his role as commander in chief. What he was unwilling to do earlier he was now compelled to do. The stakes had just been raised. If he did not attack, he would surely lose his son. For Saul it had become personal.

THIS IS ONE REASON IT IS CRITICAL TO SEIZE EVERY DIVINE MOMENT. YOU CAN NEVER KNOW AT THE ONSET ALL THAT GOD INTENDS TO DO THROUGH YOUR SIMPLE ACT OF OBEDIENCE.

A lack of urgency could cost him Jonathan's life. This is one reason it is critical to seize every divine moment. You can never know at the onset all that God intends to do through your simple act of obedience. It may be a solitary moment between you and God when you experience Him more intimately. Your field of influence may extend only to those who are directly touched by your actions. Yet most likely your influence will go far beyond.

God loves to use our faithfulness to inspire the faith of others.

With every decision to embrace the God-given potential of each day, you become more magnetic and reflective of God's character. You may remain unaware, but the hand of God on your life will become undeniable to others around you. It shouldn't surprise you that through a simple act of obedience, God would choose to shake things up and disrupt the status quo. God did that through Jonathan, and He has been doing it through men and women throughout history. And He'll do it at the most surprising times and often in the most surprising ways.

TAKING JESUS TO GODLESS PLACES

In *An Unstoppable Force* I mention one of those experiences where we saw God shake things up beyond our normal span of influence. I can describe it only as a disproportionate impact in relationship to the size of the effort. We had been at a conference where we learned that effective marketing was clearly a significant element of a church's success, but the problem was with three million people in the heart of Los Angeles and nine million people in Los Angeles County, it would take several million dollars to get one notable campaign going. At the same time we had an opportunity to start a weekend worship service in the nightclub we had rented for the last three years. The downtown SoHo is not a former nightclub, but an open and active nightclub. We could have never foreseen that one of the first guests to be invited by a guest was a journalist for the *Los Angeles Times*. Michael Luo didn't come to write a story, but was so intrigued by what was happening that he left with a story.

From his nearly full-page write-up in the Metro section of the *Los Angeles Times*, KABC News caught wind of the story. They sent television news correspondent Phillip Palmer to check out this church that worshiped in the midst of Jack Daniels and Jim

Beam. Now Jack and Jim were not available while we worshiped there, but the bar was well stocked all the same. While we were open, they were not. But when we were closed, they were definitely open. KABC liked the feature story so much that it advertised the segment throughout the week on a local radio station. The catchphrase "church in a nightclub" became the advertising mantra. To our surprise, the station also advertised with television trailers letting people know when the story would be aired. The story did so well, they decided to run it again the next week during sweeps week. In fact it was the night *Star Wars* premiered. That time they increased their marketing; we began to see billboards throughout the city with the caption, "God in a nightclub." I have to admit the trailers made me nervous. They filmed the nightclub in the midst of its activity—steamy, sensual, seductive— and then they cut quickly to our worship service, blurring the line between the two.

God was using what had been an extremely controversial decision to move into a nightclub as a way of shaking our city and letting people know that He is actively at work. I was amazed at the span of influence this one decision gave us, from an interview with New York–based *20/20*, which was curious about what was happening, to a ministry starting in a café in Wellington, New Zealand, called Mosaic.

There is a line of demarcation that those who are religious seem to establish: there are just some places they won't go and some things they won't do. Some people in our congregation were troubled when we relocated from our church sanctuary to a college auditorium. They felt we were moving from the sacred to the secular. You can only imagine the response we had when they discovered we were moving to a nightclub. If the first moved us from the sacred to the secular, this would be from the secular to the sacrilegious.

When we began our services in the nightclub, we would on occasion hand out three-by-five cards and allow those attending to write down any questions they would like addressed that evening. The first time I did this I was more than surprised by the opening question on the first card: "What is a church doing in a nightclub?" I couldn't resist responding, "What are you doing in a nightclub?" and then went on to explain that Jesus had a terrible reputation for being the friend of sinners. There is no more appropriate place for the church to be than where people need God the most. It was my hope that our decision would encourage churches around the world to risk similar ventures. We were equally committed to not being of the world and to aggressively being in the world.

> **THAT IS ONE REASON WHY THE LIFE OF JESUS IS SO COMPELLING. BEYOND HIS CLAIM TO BE GOD, THE WAY HE LIVED AS A HUMAN BEING WAS MOVING. PEOPLE WERE MAGNETIZED TO HIS LIFE. WHEN HE MOVED, THEY COULD SEE GOD.**

The irony is that often the places and the things that we eliminate are the very places Jesus visited and the things He did. His reputation was always on the line. He hung out in the wrong places with the wrong people. He was continually in the midst of the battle, never hiding under the pomegranate tree. That is one reason why the life of Jesus is so compelling. Beyond His claim to be God, the way He lived as a human being was moving. People were magnetized to His life. When He moved, they could see God.

A COMPELLING ARGUMENT

Jesus once explained to those who opposed Him that because they had seen Him, they had seen the Father. Jesus was, of course, reinforcing His divinity. To see Jesus is to see God. But the secondary application is equally profound. Jesus explained that He spoke only what He heard the Father saying and did only what He saw the Father doing. In the most concrete of ways, Jesus was saying, "Watch My life and you will see God work."

Jesus' life was an expression of the life of God, and perhaps the greatest of all miracles is that we can know this same experience. Our lives can be a response to the life of God. Imagine the power of our lives if we could know with confidence that when others see us, they would also see God; that God would reveal Himself through an ordinary human being; that those who today are blind to God would have their eyes opened by the life each of us lives. It was at Antioch that the disciples of Jesus were first called Christians. It was not a designation they gave themselves. It was the result of others observing their lives and seeing Christ in them. They looked like Jesus. Their lives reflected the adjective *Christian*. It was intended to be a description, not a title.

Paul pressed this thought even farther in Galatians 2. He declared in verse 20, "I have been crucified with Christ and I no longer live, but Christ lives in me." We are flesh-and-blood containers of the living God. We are His habitation. Our bodies are His temple and His dwelling place. And if He lives in us, whom should others see when they look into our lives? If they cannot see God, how can we claim He resides within our souls? Like Jesus, we are to live a life reflective of the

IMAGINE THE POWER OF OUR LIVES IF WE COULD KNOW WITH CONFIDENCE THAT WHEN OTHERS SEE US, THEY WOULD ALSO SEE GOD; THAT GOD WOULD REVEAL HIMSELF THROUGH AN ORDINARY HUMAN BEING; THAT THOSE WHO TODAY ARE BLIND TO GOD WOULD HAVE THEIR EYES OPENED BY THE LIFE EACH OF US LIVES.

Father. What would it be like if we spoke what we heard the Father saying and did what we saw the Father doing? Or, to put it another way, what would our lives be like if God were the Source of all our inspiration?

Marcus Gerakos is one of the most extraordinary musicians I know. He is a creator of a world music band named Escenas. He happened to live in the complex where several of the Mosaic community lived and where they had a weekly small group meeting. They would often invite Marcus to join them, but he was understandably apprehensive and occasionally dropped by when he knew the meeting was coming to a close. Several of us had the opportunity to come to know him during this period of time. For a short season I even took guitar lessons under his tutelage. It was a good way to make sure someone was meeting with him.

One of the couples he came to know was Matt and Paige. During this same period while Marcus was processing who Jesus was, Matt and Paige were preparing to move to the Middle East. They felt a specific call to work with a team that was focusing on reaching Muslims in Libya. One of Marcus's obstacles to believing in Jesus Christ was that he felt that any true religion would be all-encompassing. It would have to be global in its span of concern.

While he was struggling to believe, Matt and Paige were preparing to leave. Although the lines were invisible, there was a direct correlation between Matt and Paige's movement and Marcus's movement. When they moved toward Libya, Marcus moved toward Christ. He explained to me later that watching their commitment and the seriousness of their faith helped him move from doubt to faith. As he put it: "They take this thing really seriously, don't they?" After all, Libya is not Maui. Moving into the heart of Islam with two small daughters is not something parents do lightly. Their decision to move into the midst of the battle was a significant part of drawing Marcus into the kingdom of God.

MOVEMENT

When we move with God, we draw others into the movement. At first the activity may wake them up, and then it may unnerve them and disrupt their routine or their religious life. But in the end, for those who have ears to hear and eyes to see, they will come together and move quickly into the battle.

Maven was with them once again. He, too, was weary from the battle fought. Even in victory there is pain and death, and his thoughts traveled far beyond this moment.

He turned to Ayden and seemed to answer his thoughts: "Today we have seen a great victory, and to celebrate is a pleasure we must not neglect."

Ayden responded with joyous exuberance, "The valley of darkness is now a forest of lights!"

"Yes," Maven acknowledged. "The density of the light restrains the weight of the darkness."

"Will we settle here?" asked Kembr as she reveled in the beauty of the land.

"No," answered Maven. "The light of mankind shines only when moving forward to engage the darkness."

"Are they ready for the journey? Certainly we should stay until it is safe for them to go?" Kembr pressed.

Ayden spoke in a calming tone, "It is not the place but the presence that upholds them! This is their only certainty."

— Entry 715
The Perils of Ayden

9

AWAKENING

WAKE THE DEAD

KENTAROU NEVER HAD A CHANCE. WHAT COULD ONE person do against an entire army? He was a student of sociology at the University of Kyoto in Japan. A desire to see and experience America led him to agree to live with a family while in the States rather than stay in a hotel. His only exposure to God came from his studies, particularly the work of sociologist Max Weber. How could he know he was about to enter a mosaic of faith, love, and hope? He stayed with Gerardo and Laura Marti, and he expressed his great interest in learning the difference between Catholicism and Protestantism. Asked if he had ever read the Bible, he responded, "Never." In fact, he had never seen a Bible. In his first few days he began reading the Bible and John Eldredge's *Journey of Desire*. Two days later they introduced him to *The Jesus Film*. At the end of the film he asked with curiosity, "So Jesus is alive?" They told him yes.

He asked, "Do you have any idea where He is right now?" Like so many of us Kentarou was unaware that Jesus is right here among us through His spirit.

Gerardo then explained that Jesus is with us, actively calling and leading people to Himself.

He then met Mark and Jenea Havner, who took him out to eat Korean barbecue and introduced him to others who were also followers of Jesus Christ. And still another leader named John Wolfkill took him from the party, and they shared together as John drove him home. Kentarou was elated and shared with the Martis, "I never thought I could come to America and have such a wonderful time."

He was excited that the next day he would have an opportunity to see all his newfound friends again and experience church for the first time. He stepped into an experience filled with music, drama, dance, and what Kentarou described as human art. I had decided that morning to explain the gospel by painting one of my friends in five different colors. Kentarou explained to me after the service that I spoke English too fast for him to understand everything, but the human art made the message absolutely clear: "Jesus is alive."

On Monday Chad Becker spent the day with him, walking through the differences between Christianity and Shintoism. On Tuesday Laura's little boy Zachary took something from Kentarou's guest room, and Laura apologized on behalf of her son. His response was startling: "Of course I forgive you. I am a Christian now." He later explained that his experience within Mosaic's community brought him to faith in Jesus Christ.

On Thursday morning as he was preparing to leave for the airport, Gerardo took a few moments to ensure that Kentarou really understood what he was doing. It was clear that Kentarou believed in the person and message of Jesus Christ, but did he really understand the implications of being His follower? Gerardo explained, "What we do is pray and tell Jesus that He is our leader, that we are leaving the life when we didn't follow Him and starting a life where we do follow Him."

Immediately Kentarou put his hands together in prayer and closed his eyes in silence. Then he looked up to Gerardo and said, "Anything else?"

"Yes," Gerardo said. "You must ask Jesus to help you grow and to be a leader who tells other people about Him."

Once again he closed his eyes for a silent prayer, shortly looked up, and simply responded, "Okay."

This response caused Gerardo to start crying, and he closed the time by taking him to Matthew 28 where Jesus gave His followers the commission to go and make disciples of all nations. Gerardo explained that in the same way he was commissioned, he was now commissioning Kentarou as he was returning to Japan. Gerardo warmly looked at him and said, "Now you are my brother." And Kentarou reached out his hand toward Gerardo and responded, "Nice to meet you."

As they prayed outside the international terminal, he affirmed his new calling to reach the people of Japan. Kentarou was overwhelmed by the army of God armed with the weapons of community, truth, and creativity. Now he, too, was a warrior deployed to take the gospel to the land from which he came. Asleep within the people of God is an army waiting to be aroused. Within every individual there is potential that will never be discovered outside God's purpose.

UNLOCKING A WORLD OF POTENTIAL

"I never thought I could do that"—the wonderful words of self-discovery. Ever been thrown into the fire? No warning, no preparation, no pregame warm-up. Someone saw raw talent in you and felt it was time to squeeze it out, so he threw you into the crucible of real life, and you were going to be crushed by the moment or be reformed into a new kind of person.

Jonathans have a way of creating those kinds of environments. You follow them into a moment full of apprehension and insecurity, certain only of your inability and inadequacy, and you discover at the same time everyone else does that you were up to the challenge. You just hate those moments when they come at you, but you love them when you come out of them. It's this whole thing called potential.

There's so much talk about potential in our culture, as if it's the end-all of success. Has anyone ever said about you, "He has so much potential"? If you're under twenty—let's give you twenty-five—consider it a compliment. Potential—your untapped or unlocked capacity. Potential—the hint of greatness not yet developed. "He has so much potential"—a statement of praise and maybe even adoration. And then you're thirty, and you still have all this potential. Pressing forty, and you're still full of potential. If you're forty-five and someone looks at you and says, "You have so much potential," pause, excuse yourself, step into a closet, and have a good cry.

What once was a statement of promise is now an assessment of lost opportunity. There is a point where you're not supposed to be full of potential; you're supposed to be full of talent, capacity, product. Potential is a glimpse of what could be, yet there must be a shift from where we have potential to where we are potent.

POTENTIAL IS A GLIMPSE OF WHAT COULD BE, YET THERE MUST BE A SHIFT FROM WHERE WE HAVE POTENTIAL TO WHERE WE ARE POTENT.

Yet, as much potential as we might have, making this transition isn't all that easy. It's not one that everyone can make alone. In fact, in my estimation, no one moves from potential to maximum capacity without the help of others. Often lost potential is the result of lack of investment. This doesn't abdicate us from personal responsibility. In the end, we are responsible for our potential. It is just a reminder that our responsibility goes beyond harnessing our potential to developing the potential of others.

What began for Jonathan as a personal quest culminated in an experience of corporate greatness. Jonathan hinted at that long before it ever happened. Remember when Jonathan and his armor-bearer alone faced the Philistines, when he waited to hear what the Philistine warriors would say to him? Remember how he celebrated when they taunted him and challenged him to come up and face their wrath? Jonathan explained to his armor-bearer, "Climb up after me; the LORD has given them into the hand of Israel."

Where was Israel? Israel was everywhere but there. There was no Israel lined up behind Jonathan. He was in the battle essentially alone, just him and his youthful armor-bearer. Yet even then Jonathan understood the battle wasn't just about him. It was about all of the people of God. It was never a self-indulgent crusade. It was about fulfilling God's purpose through God's people. There would be no victory for Jonathan alone. The Lord was not delivering them into the hand of Jonathan. He was delivering them into the hand of Israel. That was what thrilled Jonathan. That brought exhilaration and hope into his spirit. He was simply the first part of the whole.

This is a difficult concept for those of us raised with a Western mind-set. The development of our nation has proved to be an unintentional experiment in individuality. Perhaps no nation has seen the individual so clearly. Our laws have not only been written around the rights and importance of the individual, but they have been shaped and reframed by a heightened individualism. Personal rights supersede the good of the whole. Communal responsibility has become virtually extinct as we have championed personal choice. We superimpose our individualistic filter on both the experiences and the people of the Scriptures.

The Bible teaches a clear sense of the uniqueness and importance of every individual. After all, each one of us has been created in the image and likeness of God. Each one of us has God's unique, divine fingerprint on his or her soul. From the Bible and biology we are overwhelmed with evidence that there are no two people who are the same. Scripture and science herald and celebrate personal uniqueness, yet this must not be confused with the worldview of individualism.

Both the Word of God and the people of God are expressive of the communal nature of our Creator. God Himself is expressed in community. He is Father, Son, and Spirit. The One who is God is expressed in three. In the mystery beyond my comprehension, God lives in perfect relationship to Himself. This aspect of God's nature is expressed through His relationality. In other words, everything He creates has a unique relationship to Himself, especially man.

God created us with the capacity for relationship, not only for relationship with Himself, but also for relationship with each other. Man was designed to live in community. When we are out of relationship, out of community, we are operating against our design. Sometimes our focus on ourselves blinds us to the intensity of our interconnectedness. How many alcoholic fathers have actually defended themselves by saying, "I'm not hurting anyone but myself"? There is no such thing. We never have the luxury of hurting only ourselves. When we hurt ourselves, others are always affected. The converse is also true. When we choose to do what is right, what is true, what is good, it always bleeds over into the lives of others.

Jonathan acted on behalf of Israel long before Israel acted on behalf of Jonathan. In the same way, those who are willing to live the adventurer's life may be required to endure great hardship for the good of the kingdom. There will be places on the adventure where you will have to stand alone. If God is using you to launch a new adventure, you may even have to bear the burden of pioneering a dangerous trail. Like Jonathan's challenge, your challenge may involve real conflict and battle. Certainly spiritual warfare is unleashed when you seize divine moments. All this was a price

Jonathan was willing to pay, not for the sake of his name, but for the sake of God's people and the name of the Lord. His sacrifice created the context to bring greatness out of others. We find in the apex of this battle at least four arenas where Jonathan's personal choice resulted in the transformation of others.

UNLEASH THE FAITHFUL

We've talked a lot about Jonathan and have virtually ignored the armor-bearer. But from the beginning the armor-bearer was with him, faithful from the start. An honest assessment of this name-less companion was that he had very little to contribute to the cause. The armor-bearer was most likely very young, inexperienced, and untrained. There is a reason why his role was to care for the armor and not to wear it. He was neither a general nor a warrior. His job was to carry the equipment. If the list had a thousand names, his name would be at the bottom.

As it was, he was the only volunteer, so he was second in command. In some ways his courage superseded Jonathan's. After all, Jonathan had a sword. I imagine he was carrying that. The armor-bearer had nothing with which to defend himself or engage the battle. And yet the account tells us that in the first attack Jonathan and his armor-bearer killed some twenty men in an area of a half acre. It is significant that the armor-bearer is highlighted. He wasn't hiding behind Jonathan or watching Jonathan go to war. Without any weaponry, with a clear disadvantage, this young apprentice was promoted to a warrior. In that moment he was translated from one who had potential to one who was potent, and without a doubt he exceeded his own expectations.

The armor-bearer reminds us that half the battle of seizing divine moments is just being there, just showing up. *Faith* is such a big word. It's exciting, daring, magnetic. *Faithful* is such an ordinary word. It is somewhat dull, routine, and bland. I'm convinced more of us would like to be known by faith, but resist the tedious journey of being faithful.

I am convinced there have been many times in my life when I experienced God's blessing and became God's instrument, not because of my talent or capacity, but because of my willingness to be there. There is a catalytic nature to moving with God. You might be surprised how many people would be willing to go with you if you would just lead the way. Move with God, invite those who have invited you to invest in their lives, and see what God would do with them.

I'M CONVINCED MORE OF US WOULD LIKE TO BE KNOWN BY FAITH, BUT RESIST THE TEDIOUS JOURNEY OF BEING FAITHFUL.

It was a Sunday morning, and Kim told me I was to pick up a young girl from church and bring her home with me. She was an illegal immigrant from Mexico, and she had no place to live. The family who had offered her a place to stay had kicked her out because she had come to know Jesus Christ. Her refusal to remain silent about her new faith cost her the only shelter she had. We were a temporary solution. She would stay with us a few days, and then we would figure out what to do. Little did we know that God intended for us, in our twenties, to become the parents of a teenager.

For the next ten years Paty lived in our home as our daughter in the Lord. She didn't speak a word of English when she began school. While attending a Christian private school, she was able to advance from kindergarten to ninth grade in one year and tenth and eleventh grades in her second year and finish high school in her third year. She graduated from Cal State Los Angeles with an education degree, and now, with her husband, Steve, and their little boy, Stevie, they are preparing to move to Indonesia to work with the Madurese people.

We didn't raise our daughter with the intended purpose of sending her to work in the Islamic world. We raised her while we were on mission. We served Paty in the name of Christ, and she in turn joined us in serving others in His name. When Paty became our daughter, she became a missionary. Becoming a part of our family was a source of security and stability. It also became the context for taking risks and living on the edge of God's kingdom movement.

When you grow up in the battle, you don't fear the war. A person who could crassly be described as an uneducated, illegal immigrant was in reality a treasure of divine potential waiting to be unleashed. She was an armor-bearer who, through her faithfulness, has become a woman of faith.

Jonathan took his armor-bearer with him because he needed him. It wasn't an act of benevolence, and he certainly wasn't trying to fill his need for companionship. The faithfulness of his armor-bearer increased his capacity to accomplish the task before him. To be faithful to his task would have been all the armor-bearer was asked to do; yet what we find is that the challenge required more of him. He followed Jonathan into the battle as an armor-bearer, but he walked out of the battle as a warrior. Though his contribution would be measured as small, the dimension of faith and courage that he demonstrated was immense. It is in the context of this demonstration of faithfulness that the armor-bearer emerged as Jonathan's right hand.

When we choose to seize divine

WHEN WE CHOOSE TO SEIZE DIVINE MOMENTS, WE CREATE AN ENVIRONMENT WHERE OTHERS ARE UNLEASHED TO FULFILL THEIR GOD-GIVEN POTENTIAL.

moments, we create an environment where others are unleashed to fulfill their God-given potential. I'm sure that many of us have experienced this phenomenon from the other side. We have been armor-bearers who have followed Jonathans where we would not have gone alone. We made a decision to serve someone else, and in serving we experienced God's best for us.

I had been a follower of Christ only a year when I was at the University of North Carolina at Chapel Hill, and a college friend invited me to visit a small church in the country. It was quite a stretch to go from a childhood in Miami to a congregation called Mount Moriah Baptist Church. Instead of concrete streets and high-rises, there were farms and horses, yet there was something wonderfully compelling about the genuineness and warmth of the people. Knowing very little about how church life worked, I approached the pastor and explained to him that I was going home for the summer, but would be back in the fall. I went on to ask him if the church had any need for a volunteer janitor. It didn't occur to me that someone would be paid to do this kind of job in a religious context, so I figured someone would need to do it.

I was so surprised two months later to receive a letter from the pastor inviting me to preach on a Sunday morning when I returned to school. In our brief conversations, I had shared my sense of calling to preach the gospel, but never expected that he would entrust me with that kind of responsibility. He didn't know me from Adam. I had never spoken in any formal or public setting. I had only asked if they needed someone to clean the building. It was Bob Weatherly, who, like a Jonathan, forced me to face challenges I did not think I was ready for.

I felt very much like an armor-bearer who did not have a weapon and wouldn't know what to do with it if he had one. I was so afraid that my message would not be biblical that I used more than 150 verses in that one talk. More than giving me an opportunity to speak, Pastor Bob taught me about servant leadership.

He modeled that you look for a person who is willing to take on the lowly tasks and develop him in his God-given potential.

When I worked in Dallas as a metropolitan consultant, I developed an internship program where young leaders would have an opportunity to develop their gifts and skills. This project called Priority One was one of my favorite and most enjoyable experiences. Yet inevitably the most enthusiastic and ambitious in the program would ask me the same question, "How can I get your job?" The question was always informed with the subtle belief that most things are political. I must confess that a part of my disappointment in my spiritual journey has been the secular nature of so much Christian work. My answer was always the same. I'd simply tell them, "I don't know how somebody else would get this job, but for me, I spent ten years of my life working among the poor." And then I would ask them, "Do you want the outcome without the journey? Because if that's the case, I don't know how to tell you to get there."

Jonathans get their names in the book; armor-bearers are anonymous. We should never confuse anonymity with insignificance. Perhaps a more real picture is that many of us are at times armor-bearers and at other times Jonathans. An honest look at the most successful life would in humility acknowledge that many Jonathans—those men and women who through their lives created the environment where another was called to greatness—were in that one's life. At the same time each of us, through our own sacrifice, can not only inspire but also empower others to achieve great things for God.

IGNITE THE APATHETIC

The passage tells us that the armor-bearer became a warrior, and it also informs us that Saul and all of his men assembled and went into the battle. We find that Jonathans not only create an environment where the faithful are unleashed, but they also, through their initiative, cause the paralyzed to be mobilized. From one perspective it would be easy to conclude that Jonathan was moving too fast, yet the truth is that any speed of progress looks like blinding speed when everyone else is standing still.

Saul was not about to attack. He was not going to call his army to move forward and engage the enemy. Saul and his men had lost heart. They were apathetic. They had lost their passion. In Romans 10:2 the apostle Paul reminded us of the danger of zeal without knowledge; King Saul reminded us of the tragedy of knowledge without zeal. Only the commotion of the conflict shook Saul out of his complacency. Certainly the fact that the one who was missing was his son had to make a difference.

Saul didn't care about much other than himself, but Jonathan he loved. I wonder: *If the missing soldier had been anyone else, would Saul have been moved at all?* But now it was personal. His son Jonathan was at war. The son of the king was doing what the king should have been doing. All of his excuses fell empty. He had only a sword. That's all his son had. He had only a few hundred men. Jonathan had but one.

The moment Saul chose to advance found no improvement on his previous dilemma. They were not in a better situation. They did not have more weapons. There were no reinforcements. If anything, his ammunition had just been reduced by 50 percent. He had just lost his most fierce warrior. His leadership was divided,

> WE FIND THAT JONATHANS NOT ONLY CREATE AN ENVIRONMENT WHERE THE FAITHFUL ARE UNLEASHED, BUT THEY ALSO, THROUGH THEIR INITIATIVE, CAUSE THE PARALYZED TO BE MOBILIZED.

and the Philistines were alerted to their coming. The situation wasn't better, but the stakes had changed. There was someone involved that Saul cared about. For his son he was willing to risk his life and the lives of his men. For his son he was willing to go to war. If the rational thing to do was to avoid conflict with the Philistines, engaging them at that point was absolutely insane.

It is easy to make decisions that are objective and rational when you're not personally involved. When you become connected at a heart level, your base of information changes. This is the power of passion, of caring about something or someone. Jonathan's action fueled in Saul what had remained unignited. In the same way, when we seize divine moments, we ignite a context in which the apathetic are impassioned.

I recently sat in a meeting filled with the leaders of numerous parachurch ministries. We were invited to work together for the purpose of creating an event that would serve pastors across the nation. On the second day we had an interesting dialogue about the relationship between the local church and what was uncomfortably described as the parachurch. As I looked around the room, I made the observation that the organizations that were represented at the table were a reflection of the apathy of the local church. Parachurches emerged in response to the paralysis within the local church. The passion that fuels these cause-oriented organizations stands as an indictment against the apathy of many of our congregations.

Dr. Keith Phillips, the founder of World Impact, was among the group. His responses to my comments have remained with me since. He explained that in his own experience growing up in Los Angeles, this was exactly right. His summary was that World Impact was created to start churches among poor people because the church didn't care enough to go. We have a lot of great assemblies that we call churches, yet the very word *church* means "to be called out." No football team has ever won a Super Bowl on the strength of the huddle. It's what happens after the "ready, break" that brings the victory. Saul and all his men assembled and went into battle. Like Israel's army, you cannot win a war until you leave the assembly and engage the battle. It's not enough to assemble; you also have to go to war.

We have a propensity toward assembling for our own good without being moved to serve the good of others. Jonathans break the cycle of self-indulgence. They give their lives away passionately, and through the magnetism of their own lives, they move hearts that have long gone still.

RECLAIM THE REBELLIOUS

The passage goes on to tell us that "those Hebrews who had previously been with the Philistines and had gone up with them to their camp went over to the Israelites who were with Saul and Jonathan." If it were not difficult enough for Jonathan to have to work against the apathy of his father and his men, he had to face the reality that many of their own had turned against them. There were traitors in the camp. They had weighed the Israelites and the Philistines and found the people of God wanting.

For some people being on the right side is about what is right, but for others being on the right side means making sure you win. We certainly live in a culture that glamorizes whoever wins regardless of character. You can have a criminal record and live an unsavory and notorious life, but if you win the Super Bowl, you're the hero. We've convinced ourselves that the content of a person's character has nothing to do with his effectiveness or stature.

There were Israelites who were willing to war against the very purpose of God to ensure their personal survival and success. They walked away from what they knew was right and became enemies of the good. Yet in that moment everything changed for them. When they saw Jonathan and Saul battling the Philistines, facing insurmountable odds without retreat, something happened. They remembered who they were. This is perhaps one of the most satisfying benefits of seizing a divine opportunity. Not only are the faithful unleashed and the paralyzed mobilized, but often we find to our delight, to God's pleasure, that prodigals are restored.

Two years ago a young couple walked into our church on Sunday morning. They stood out for a number of reasons, one of which was that they made their way to the front just to find me and say hello. They both seemed bright, energetic, and extremely enthusiastic about being there that day. Colin Johnson and Shiho Inoue were at the same time living together and searching for God. They were a contradiction of terms in that Colin grew up in a Christian home and had tremendous disdain for the church and Shiho grew up in a Japanese home without any teaching about God and had an unexplainable attraction to Jesus.

Colin's earring, nose ring, and tongue ring somehow didn't seem to match the culture of a child whose parents had master's degrees from Regents University, the school founded by Pat Robertson. At first glance you would conclude that Colin was a classically unchurched university student, yet the reality was quite the opposite. He had become quite comfortable with being identified with one camp while working for the other. Even while he was worshiping with us in San Gabriel, he was dealing drugs on the west side. He was one of perhaps millions in our Western society who had learned to live within a religion without experiencing transformation. In some ways you could say that Colin was a Christian who did not know Christ. Yet in the end their quest for God proved to be genuine. If there was a God to know, they wanted to meet Him.

Soon both Colin and Shiho became followers of Christ, yet

Colin's defining moment may have come in one particular con-versation. Even after coming to faith Colin was an extremely bright guy who always looked for loopholes. A range of issues such as moving to a life of moral purity created a real crisis for Colin. Colin could take a clear teaching in the Bible and make it obscure for his own purpose. All the arguments in the world really did not have a significant impact until one day at the end of a conversation with his mentor, Mike Tafoya. As he was walk-ing out the door, Mike stopped him with one last thought: "Colin, you're radical about everything else. Why don't you become radical for Jesus?" Colin said that was the moment when everything changed.

That one thought made everything clear. The compelling rea-son he was looking for to live his life differently was right in front of him. Religion just wasn't enough to change Colin's life. The fear of consequence or the opinions of others were not adequate moti-vations to change his priorities. The call to be a good person just wasn't that compelling. Colin was anti-institution, and if any-thing, he was resistant to conforming to expectations of others. It was the movement that captured him—that something important was happening in the world, that God, through His Son, Jesus Christ, had started a revolution and was inviting him to join. No observers invited, no spectators necessary, only revolutionaries, only radicals need apply.

This is the power that draws the prodigal back home. When someone has chosen to walk away from God or God's people, polite religion will not be enough to draw him back. There are thousands upon thousands who may never again step through the doors of any religious institution, and they openly explain, "I've already tried that." The individual who has rejected religion and is living like hell will not be won back except by those who are liv-ing like heaven.

I often hear the criticism that large churches are full of Christians taken from smaller churches. This is considered an indictment of their integrity and genuine spirituality. Perhaps this is rooted in the assumption of why people leave one church and go to another. If you leave to access the conveniences of the larger church, then consumerism might be the inappropriate motivator. But I think many have made these choices for other reasons. People are desperately longing to be a part of something that's making a difference. We all want, in some small way, to be a part of changing the world. I have to wonder: *How many of those people who joined a fast-growing church were not drawn to the compelling movement of Christ?* A people alive and moving with God are a compelling force. If people need to leave Mosaic to connect to God more deeply, then what I need to do is help Mosaic change. It has taken me awhile, but I've come to realize that one of the evidences of life in our community is that those who walked away have been brought back by what God is doing in our midst. God celebrates every time a prodigal returns home. Jonathans create environments that win back the hearts of the ones who have lost them.

WE ALL WANT, IN SOME SMALL WAY, TO BE A PART OF CHANGING THE WORLD.

Samuel gave us one final description of those who were moved by Jonathan's actions: "When all the Israelites who had hidden in the hill country of Ephraim heard that the Philistines were on the run, they joined the battle in hot pursuit." Jonathan's armor-bearer followed him when there seemed to be no hope of success. Saul engaged the battle with his men only after he knew Jonathan was at war. Those who had walked away from God's people returned only after they saw Jonathan, Saul, and all the army attacking the Philistines.

HEAL THE BROKEN

One other group joined the battle. If all the rest came in a bit late, this group brought up the rear. A whole colony of Israelites were hiding in the hills. They were living in fear of the Philistines and had chosen to crawl into holes. The account tells us only after the Philistines were on the run did that group pop its head out and join the battle. If the first group could be described as the faithful, the second as the paralyzed, and the third as prodigals, the last would be best described as the dysfunctional. They illustrate well those who are emotionally and spiritually broken, unable to live a life of freedom and adventure. In this particular situation they were hiding in the hills, living like animals, paralyzed by fear. Today they would be described as phobic. *Phobia* is just a contemporary word for "fear." When you are controlled by a phobia, you are controlled by a specific fear. Claustrophobia is the fear of enclosed places; xenophobia, the fear of strangers; arachnophobia, the fear of spiders—you get the idea.

Now all of us deal with fear. There is nothing necessarily unhealthy about the emotion of fear. And if we're in genuine danger, it might be dysfunctional to have no fear at all. But when fear controls our lives, it is appropriate to say we are dysfunctional. Those Israelites were living in bondage. They were captives to their fear. They had made themselves useless and irrelevant to the cause. They had placed their own security above the good of the whole. They didn't want to face the problems; they were unwilling to make any sacrifice to solve the problems; they were willing to run and hide and leave the future in the hands of others. If the Philistines were to prevail, they would die in exile, be executed by their enemies, or at best live as prisoners. If the Israelites prevailed, you would think their outcome would be good, but in fact that is unlikely. If they returned to a land conquered by the Israelites, if they came down from the hillsides after there was no longer the danger of the Philistines, they would still have to face their greatest enemy.

Whatever existed within them that caused them to live a life dominated by fear would remain. Whatever was lacking in the core of their character would still mark the center of a hollow shell. If they returned to live a life of prosperity without having taken the journey of sacrifice, they themselves would become the new enemies of Israel. God could have easily removed the Philistines without Israel going to war, but He could not make Israel the people He needed if they would not fight on His behalf.

God uses the challenges we face to shape the character within us. Power without humility is a bad combination. Wealth without generosity is equally dangerous. Freedom without faith and faithfulness will lead only to corruption and death. God wasn't just freeing the land; God was shaping the people. We are our own worst enemies when our hearts are left unattended. To miss the battle is to lose the ability to fully enjoy the victory. It is not simply battles that are won, but fear that is conquered. Divine moments compel us to live differently, and this different life that we are called to live requires us to become different.

Over the past twenty years I have walked the hill country of Ephraim. All around me I have met men, women, and children who are hiding in the hills. The fragmentation of everyday people has moved to a point of devastation. The belief that people can actually live healthy and whole lives has almost lost its merit. Even churches are overwhelmed by the pain and brokenness they face in their communities. From clergy to psychotherapists, we are a society struggling to discover how to help people get better. There is a window of hope in this passage of Scripture. They didn't step up at first, and it took them awhile to respond; it was only after the Philistines were on the run. But still, in the end, those who were living like animals, hiding from the realities of the world around them, those who were more haunted by fear than threat, joined in the battle. Samuel seemed to enjoy this description, telling us that they joined the battle in hot pursuit.

It is a powerful thing when you give yourself away to a higher purpose. There is a healing nature in joining a greater good. Recent studies are showing that people who believe in God actually live healthier lives. This fact shouldn't surprise any of us. While it's important to take care of yourself, it is extremely dangerous to make yourself all you care about. It does matter that the Israelites who were hidden away engaged in the battle. Their ability to enjoy the benefit of the peace that would eventually result is directly related to their participation. Simply translated, we get better when we give ourselves away.

This is a part of the power and blessing of the church, to bring personal and communal health. When the church moves with God, the broken are drawn to God and find healing within the movement. When we, like Christ, begin to serve others in His name, we discover that our needs have been met in the process. When the people of God relinquish the purpose of God, when there is no movement, we lose the power to change lives.

WHEN THE CHURCH MOVES WITH GOD, THE BROKEN ARE DRAWN TO GOD AND FIND HEALING WITHIN THE MOVEMENT.

Each of us has the power to create environments where the broken are made whole. Divine moments are not self-serving gifts from God; they are invitations from God to give yourself away in serving. For those who choose this path, they find their greatest joy when they bring greatness out of others. The ministry of Jesus was affirmed to John the Baptist. Through those signs the blind received sight, the lame walked, those who had leprosy were cured, the deaf heard, the dead were raised, and the good news was preached to the poor. Everywhere Jesus went, with every person who followed Him, people got better. It should not surprise us that this would be the end result when we choose to seize divine moments.

RAISE THE DEAD

It would be easy to conclude that the world would be a better place if it wasn't for people, that the church would be a better place if it wasn't for Christians. You might make the mistake of thinking that your journey with God would find its greatest fulfillment if you could remove the human obstacle—people. Yet the journey is lived out in the context of relationships, and a significant part of the adventure is the way that God uses you in the lives of others. If you have ever dared to love deeply, then you have been deeply disappointed. We are all broken vessels with divine capacity. A part of the challenge is to never give up on people.

Jesus refused to give up on us. He was not unclear concerning our condition. He knew we were not simply sick; He could see that we were dead. Yet His death and resurrection remain the divine declaration that we, too, can live. God came to raise the dead. Do you believe that God could do the same through you? Only Jesus could die for the sins of the world. Yet in a marvelous way God uses those who would go on His behalf to speak life into the dead.

It was this kind of vision that God gave to Ezekiel. In chapter 37 of his journal, Ezekiel wrote this account:

The hand of the LORD was upon me, and he brought me out by the Spirit of the LORD and set me in the middle of a valley; it was full of bones. He led me back and forth among them, and I saw a great many bones on the floor of the valley, bones that were very dry. He asked me, "Son of man, can these bones live?"

I said, "O Sovereign LORD, you alone know."

Then he said to me, "Prophesy to these bones and say to them, 'Dry bones, hear the word of the LORD! This is what the Sovereign LORD says to these bones: I will make breath enter you, and you will come to life. I will attach tendons to you and make flesh come upon you and cover you with skin; I will put breath in you, and you will come to life. Then you will know that I am the LORD.'"

So I prophesied as I was commanded. And as I was prophesying, there was a noise, a rattling sound, and the bones came together, bone to bone. I looked, and tendons and flesh appeared on them and skin covered them, but there was no breath in them.

Then he said to me, "Prophesy to the breath; prophesy, son of man, and say to it, 'This is what the Sovereign LORD says: Come from the four winds, O breath, and breathe into these slain, that they may live.'" So I prophesied as he commanded me, and breath entered them; they came to life and stood up on their feet—a vast army. (vv. 1–10)

A valley of dry bones transformed into a vast army of God. This is the vision that challenges our faith. This is the promise that God brings to us and then through us. What may be beyond your imagination—that a cemetery could become a maternity ward—is the greatest reward of the Jonathan Factor. God longs to use you to bring hope to those who have essentially gone to an early grave. When you move with God, you begin to raise the dead. The primary symbols of the Christian faith—the cross, baptism, and the Lord's Supper—are all declarations that through sacrifice comes life.

After showing him this vision, God explained to Ezekiel,

Son of man, these bones are the whole house of Israel. They say, "Our bones are dried up and our hope is gone; we are cut off." Therefore prophesy and say to them: "This is what the Sovereign LORD says:

O my people, I am going to open your graves and bring you up from them; I will bring you back to the land of Israel. Then you, my people, will know that I am the LORD, when I open your graves and bring you up from them. I will put my Spirit in you and you will live, and I will settle you in your own land. Then you will know that I the LORD have spoken, and I have done it." (Ezek. 37:11–14)

God is always the Source of life. Wherever He is, there is always a future and a hope. He raises us from the dead, never intending that we would spend our lives leaning against our tombstones. Too many of us have pitched our tents in the cemetery next to the church. He speaks life into our dry bones so that we would become the vast army of God. To know the life of God is to follow Him into this new frontier. To know His power is to walk through this valley of the dead, and with every step feel the four winds come and breathe life into the multitudes. As He did with Jonathan, God uses us to unleash an army.

MOVING ON

The passage closes with this last thought: "So the LORD rescued Israel that day, and the battle moved on beyond Beth Aven," which is a good reminder to all of us that no matter how profound or dramatic a divine moment may be, no matter its significance or its breadth of impact, even if at the end of the day we are able to look back and reflect on the amazing experience we have just encountered, we must never forget that the battle moves on. With the end of each day, there is a promise of another day's coming. And with that new day come new battles, new opportunities, new challenges, new adventures. Even while we celebrate the last moment's victory, we begin the new moment's journey. We must engage it with fresh energy and anticipation.

You know where to begin: take initiative. You know who God is, so embrace life's uncertainty. Remember that the person you are becoming in Jesus Christ is your greatest gift to others, so use your influence. Every great adventure is filled with peril and danger, but the risk is worth it. You have already been authorized to move forward, so advance. Impact your world by fighting the battles that are on God's heart. Move with an urgency that creates a movement. Engage in an adventure so compelling that it causes the awakening of the dead in spirit. In this moment, each of us will have to choose. Will you seize the power of every moment or let them slip away?

> **YOU KNOW WHERE TO BEGIN: TAKE INITIATIVE. YOU KNOW WHO GOD IS, SO EMBRACE LIFE'S UNCERTAINTY.**

A man stood blind before Jesus and His disciples. All they could think to do was to have a meaningless conversation about whose fault it was that he was blind. The man was blind, but he wasn't deaf. He could hear the callousness of their conversation. They were oblivious to the fact that they were the ones most blind—blind to his pain, to his disappointment, to his need. Jesus rebuked their insensitivity and lack of compassion. They were friends of God and still could not see the extraordinary opportunity awaiting them. Somehow alleviating human suffering just didn't seem that urgent. It seemed far more important to engage God in a philosophical discussion.

This moment was far too important to Jesus. It must not be missed. He uses this moment to open their eyes to what is clearly an unseen reality. God is at work. Even if we don't care about humanity, He does. Every human being matters to Him. Even this man's blindness cannot stop God from doing something extraordinary in and through his life. Right now it is God's desire that His purpose might be displayed through this man's life. And then He challenges them, "As long as it is day, we must do the work of Him who sent me. Night is coming, when no one can work. While I'm in the world, I am the light of the world." In other words, stop wasting time and start chasing daylight.

Remember, it just takes one moment to change everything.

Now I say this, brethren, that flesh and blood cannot inherit the kingdom of God; nor does the perishable inherit the imperishable. Behold, I tell you a mystery; we will not all sleep, but we will all be changed, *in a moment,* in the twinkling of an eye, at the last trumpet; for the trumpet will sound, and the dead will be raised imperishable, and we will be changed. For this perishable must put on the imperishable, and this mortal must put on immortality. But when this perishable will have put on the imperishable, and this mortal will have put on immortality, then will come about the saying that is written, "DEATH IS SWALLOWED UP in victory. O DEATH, WHERE IS YOUR VICTORY? O DEATH, WHERE IS YOUR STING?" The sting of death is sin, and the power of sin is the law; but thanks be to God, who gives us the victory through our Lord Jesus Christ. Therefore, my beloved brethren, be steadfast, immovable, always abounding in the work of the Lord, knowing that your toil is not in vain in the Lord. (1 Cor. 15:50–58 NASB, italics added)

ABOUT THE AUTHOR

ERWIN RAPHAEL MCMANUS IS LEAD PASTOR AND cultural architect of Mosaic, a uniquely innovative, international congregation in Los Angeles. He is a national and international strategist and communicator on culture, change, creativity, and leadership. His work is featured in numerous films, articles, and magazines across the US and internationally. He also partners with Bethel Theological Seminary as a distinguished lecturer and futurist.

Erwin is the catalyst behind Awaken, a collaboration of entrepreneurs committed to creating environments that expand imagination and unleash creativity. Convinced that the world is changed by dreamers and visionaries, Awaken serves humanity through its commitment to maximize the creative potential in every individual and organization.

His first book, *An Unstoppable Force*, was a 2002 ECPA Gold Medallion Award finalist. He is also author of *Seizing Your Divine Moment, Uprising: A Revolution of the Soul* (also companion *The Uprising Experience* life storyboard), *The Barbarian Way*, and *Soul Cravings*, soon to be released in 2006.

Erwin is a native of El Salvador. He and his wife, Kim, have two children, Aaron and Mariah, and a daughter in the Lord, Paty.

AWAKEN

To learn more about living
the Awakened Life go to

www.awakenhumanity.org